# UNLOCKING THE SCRIPTURES

THE KEY TO INDUCTIVE BIBLE STUDY

by

**CYRIL J. BARBER**

*Foreword by Dr. Warren W. Wiersbe*

*Wipf & Stock*
PUBLISHERS
*Eugene, Oregon*

Wipf and Stock Publishers
199 West 8th Avenue, Suite 3
Eugene, Oregon 97401

Unlocking the Scriptures
The Key to Inductive Bible Study
By Barber, Cyril J.
Copyright©2001 by Barber, Cyril J.
ISBN: 1-59244-575-6
Publication date 3/4/2004
Previously published by Promise Publishing, 2001

Scripture quotations identified as NIV are taken from the Holy Bible, New International Version. Copyright © 1973, 1978, 1984 by International Bible society. Used by permission of Zondervan Publishing House. All rights reserved.

Scripture quotations identified as NKJV have been taken from the New King James Version of the Bible. © 1979, 1980, 1982, by Thomas Nelson, Inc., Publishers. All rights reserved.

Other quotations of Scripture are taken from the New American Standard Bible © 1960, 1962, 1963, 1968, 1971, 1972, 1973, 1975, and 1977 by The Lockman Foundation, and are used by permission.

Paraphrases of Scripture are the author's.

**Dedicated to My Grandchildren**

*Stephen Jr., Jennifer, Jonathan, Scott, and Joanne*

## CONTENTS

FOREWORD by Warren W. Wiersbe

PREFACE

| | | |
|---|---|---|
| 1. | Biblical Investigation | 1 |
| 2. | The Importance of Accuracy | 17 |
| 3. | Feast of Joy | 31 |
| 4. | On the Right Track | 49 |
| 5. | Love Letters | 71 |
| 6. | Window On the World | 87 |
| 7. | Spanning the Centuries | 103 |
| 8. | At the Center | 117 |
| 9. | Roots, Relationships and Responsibility | 129 |
| 10. | Learning About People, Part 1 | 143 |
| 11. | Learning About People, Part 2 | 159 |
| 12. | The Connection Between Being and Doing | 175 |
| 13. | The Goal of Life | 189 |
| 14. | Reaping the Rewards | 203 |
| 15. | The Finale | 213 |

## FOREWORD

Numerous books are available to help us in our study of the Bible, and most of them are useful in one way or another. Some give us a list of rules to obey while others major on discussing principles or focusing on examples. Very few of them do what this book does: teach us how to study God's Word by walking us through a specific context and showing us how to discover its riches.

That specific context is the life of Abraham and Sarah, a foundational biography in Scripture. If we want to understand God's dealings with Israel and the Church, His plan of salvation and how to have a life of faith, we must start with Abraham and Sarah.

These pages don't so much lecture us on what to do as much as to help us do it. As we read with the Bible before us, we find ourselves mining treasures of truth and having the joy of finding them for ourselves. At the same time, because we remain in one context, we get to see more clearly the development of doctrinal and practical truth in God's Word. *There's nothing more valuable to the serious Bible student than seeing the unity of God's Word and its practical application to everyday life.*

We should find ourselves growing in our own spiritual life as we walk with Abraham and Sarah. After all, what good is it to become an expert Bible student if we aren't becoming better Christians? Peter exhorts us to grow in grace as well as in knowledge (II Peter 3:18), and this book encourages both. For that reason I recommend this book to seasoned saints as well as to young believers. I wish I had read a book like this when I started my own Christian walk and ministry.

One word of caution: no speed-reading! It's not that kind of book. The words of the *Book of Common Prayer* apply to Scripture—this is a book to "read, mark, learn, and inwardly digest." If you do, you'll be able to "read, mark, learn, and inwardly digest" your Bible and grow in Christian character and service.

After all, you're not just holding a book. You're holding a key that can help you open the doors of Holy Scripture and make exciting discoveries that will result in your worshipping God more and serving Him better.

Warren W. Wiersbe

Author and Conference Speaker.

## PREFACE

Soon after my family and I moved to Southern California, we began visiting different places of interest. We were awe-struck at the beauty of Yosemite, the Sequoias, and King's Canyon; we also traveled north along the Pacific Coast Highway, and in the course of time, we followed signs that led us over bumpy roads to ghost towns and played-out gold mines. Some of these old mining towns took visitors on tours and even invited them to take off their shoes, roll up their slacks (unless, of course, they were wearing shorts), step into a cold, mountain stream and pan for gold. Each person was given a pan and showed how to scoop up some gravel from the stream and swirl it around so that centrifugal force gradually spun the gravel over the edge of the pan, leaving tiny flecks of gold behind. Our sons had not yet reached their teen years and this experience became one of the high points of their vacation.[1]

Bible study is like panning for gold. It requires diligence, an easy-to-learn technique, and perseverance. In the end, however, one's efforts are handsomely rewarded.

But why is so much stress placed on Bible study? Dr. Charles C. Ryrie in his Introduction to the *Ryrie Study Bible* wrote: **"The Bible is the greatest of all books; to study it is the noblest of all pursuits; to understand it, the highest of all goals."** This statement deserves to be written out on a card and placed on one's desk where it can serve as a continual reminder of the challenge that faces each one

---

[1] A variation of this is the underwater search for long-lost treasure. When a shipwreck has been located one of the commonest procedures is to dredge the bottom. Whatever is siphoned from the ocean bed is then strained through a sieve at the surface.

of us every day. According to Hebrews 5:13-14 a knowledge of the Bible is also the means of spiritual growth and contributes to our discernment of good and evil.

Four decades ago, I had the privilege of studying under Dr. Howard G. Hendricks of the Dallas Theological Seminary. Two of the courses I took from him focused on Bible study. The first was basic in nature. Dr. Hendricks used different portions of the Bible to illustrate for us how to analyze different types of biblical literature. The second course was based on the Book of Nehemiah and concentrated on Bible analysis. Both of these courses enriched my life immeasurably and laid a solid foundation for my own study and teaching of God's Word.

This book is based on the life and times of Abraham. As *"the father of the faithful"* his life is worthy of serious study. Abraham is mentioned in 28 books of the Bible, and numerous works have been written about him. This book differs from those presently available, for it explains to readers *how* they may study the Bible for themselves while also giving them information about the patriarch.

For several years I have had the privilege of teaching adults in churches in Southern California, most recently in the Plymouth Church, Whittier. My presentation has always been non-technical, practical, and devotional. I trust this book captures the essence of those hands-on situations.

Special thanks is due to two people who have helped bring this work to completion: Mrs. Kevin (Jan) Hussey carefully edited the manuscript, and my dear friend, Dr. Warren W. Wiersbe kindly wrote the Foreword. To them I say a very sincere "Thank you!

Cyril J. Barber

Chapter One

# BIBLICAL INVESTIGATION

One of my favorite TV shows is the "National Geographic Explorer." Of all the programs I've watched on the "Explorer," the one that fascinated me the most was *Atocha: Quest for Treasure*. The documentary focuses on Mel Fisher and his family. They live on the island of Key West, Florida. During his lifetime Mel has been a chicken farmer and Jack-of-all-trades. His claim to fame, however, arises from his discovery of the *Atocha*.

Called officially *Nuestra Senora de Atocha*, this Spanish galleon is reputed to have been the wealthiest treasure ship ever to sail the Spanish Main. Early in September 1622 the *Atocha*, together with the *Santa Margarita* and a flotilla of smaller ships, prepared to leave Havana, Cuba, for Spain. The *Atocha* carried a staggering cargo estimated at over 40 tons of gold and silver along with the biggest cache of emeralds and other gems ever assembled. Its overall value is impossible to estimate, though some have projected it to be between $100 million and $400 million dollars.

On September 4, the ships set sail. In addition to her cargo, the *Atocha* had 265 passengers. All were happy to be leaving the hardships of the New World for the gaiety and sophistication of their Iberian homeland. Less than 48 hours into the voyage, however, a mighty hurricane swept westward across the Atlantic. The tiny cluster of ships was driven inexorably toward the Florida reefs. The *Santa Margarita* was the first to sink. Within hours the *Atocha* followed. Their demise was witnessed by a few survivors from some of the smaller vessels.

Over the years, many treasure seekers have looked for the *Santa Margarita* and the *Atocha*, hoping to become rich overnight. These adventurers have found artifacts from other wrecks, but the location of the *Santa Margarita* and *Atocha* remained a mystery.

Someone, however, is sure to ask, "What does all of this have to do with Bible study?" In one of his hymns of praise, David described the unsurpassed excellence of God's Word, and concluded by saying that a knowledge of Scripture is *"more desirable than gold, yes, than much fine gold"* (Psalm 19:7-10). Ironically, the principles of a rewarding study of Scripture are illustrated for us in the *procedures* Mel Fisher and his crew followed as they searched for the *Atocha*. And these procedures have been confirmed in the experiences of those who penned God's inspired Word (cf. Psalm 119:72, 127).

The Fishers' search began in earnest in 1970 when a researcher in a library in Seville, Spain, accidentally came across a reference to the possible whereabouts of the *Atocha*—the Marquises Keys off the coast of Florida. He contacted Mel Fisher who immediately rounded up a team of divers and scientists, and they set out in search of the lost ship.

But where would they begin to look? Numerous islands make up the Marquises, and the sea around them covers a vast area. How would they know if they were in the right vicinity?

It took Mel Fisher and his team many years of hard work—covering 120,000 linear miles of ocean—before they found an anchor that indicated they were in the general area where the *Atocha* sank. This was followed by cluster upon cluster of silver coins. Then, three silver bars. Finally, using a magnetometer, they found other evidences of the *Atocha's* cargo. Even then, it was many months before they located what they had come to refer to as the "mother lode." In all, Mel Fisher and his crew spent sixteen years in their search. Ultimately, with the discovery of the gold, they were rewarded with wealth beyond their fondest dreams.

A study of the Bible is similar to the quest for the *Atocha*, only infinitely more rewarding. God uses many metaphors to describe the value of the revelation He has given to us. As we have noted, in Psalm 19:10, He compares His Word to *"priceless gold,"* and in Proverbs 2:4, He likens the wisdom to be found within its pages as *"hidden treasure."*[1] The New Testament continues this idea of accumulated riches and states that it is the responsibility of every believer to know the Word of God so well that he[2] is able to impart to others truths that are

---

[1] These illustrations do not exhaust the metaphors used to describe the Bible or the value of its study. Cf. Psalm 119:105; John 17:17*b*; etc.

[2] I am aware of the fact that, in general, women are more diligent in their study of the Bible than men. At Plymouth Church in Whittier we have a dozen week-day Bible study groups started by women, one for men and women, but only one for men. Sundays, of course, are different. Women, therefore, are to be commended for their devotion, and men need to be encouraged to take up a serious study of God's Word either on their own or in a group.

both new and old (Matthew 13:52; see also II Timothy 2:2, 15; 3:17; 4:4).

The story told by the National Geographic Society in 60 minutes is fascinating, but the search itself involved hours spent in libraries poring over ancient maps, consulting ships' logs, scanning old weather tables, studying ships' manifests, and comparing these with other recorded finds—and all with a view to uncovering the slightest clue that could lead to the place where a ship's cargo lay concealed on the ocean floor. It was laborious, painstaking work, often requiring a knowledge of one or more foreign language. And every bit of relevant information had to be cataloged and filed against the day when it might be the one clue that would lead to the resting-place of the *Atocha*.

The more work that went into the preparation of the expedition, the greater was the anticipation on the part of the underwater treasure-seekers. They became impatient to get under way. Locating the site of a wreck, however, was like piecing together a very large complex jigsaw puzzle.

Underwater investigators use different strategies to locate a wrecked ship. Magnetometers are useful when one is down on the ocean floor or if the water is shallow, but they are not as useful when trying to scan a vast area. What a diver must look for, therefore, are clues to the whereabouts of a sunken vessel. Coral, for example, grows in haphazard clusters. Evidence that there is something unusual beneath is indicated by a coral encrustation that follows the outline of a ship's hull or takes on the shape of an anchor or a cannon.

Other divers have experimented with hot air balloons. They ascend a hundred feet or more above the ocean and eagerly scan the depths beneath them. This is a helpful method, but only if the water is clear, for it enables a would-be salvager to survey a greater area than would be possible if he were underwater. If the murkiness of the water limits visibility, then other strategies have to be used. In such instances, some divers have resorted to being pulled along in a cage behind a motorboat. Even so, the principle is the same. They look for anything that follows a pattern or is in a straight line.

Ships that sailed the open seas often used ballast for stability. When swept along by a hurricane, the hull might be ripped open by a submerged reef. The ship would not sink immediately, but the ballast would begin to tumble out. It would fall to the ocean floor and leave (for the watchful observer) a line of evidence that would lead to the final resting-place of the one-time seaworthy vessel.

These techniques used by underwater explorers make sense, and similar strategies are employed when we study God's Word. Not all portions of God's Word are the same. We begin with an overview and then gradually narrow our search using different techniques. Of course, there is also a more immediate reward in Bible study. When compared with the thousands of treasure seekers, many of whom spend their entire life's savings looking for sunken riches (with only a few finding what they were looking for), *all who study into God's Word are rewarded* (cf. Psalm 119:97, 103-04). Jeremiah, for example, said, *"Your words were found and I ate them, and Your words became for me a joy and the delight of my heart"* (Jeremiah 15:16). His deepest needs were met, and his hunger for knowledge and understanding was satisfied.

## CAREFUL OBSERVATION

To study the Word of God successfully so that we may experience what Jeremiah enjoyed, we need to develop the same passion and commitment as the underwater treasure-seekers. We also need to develop certain skills and techniques. These begin with *observation*,[3] when we ask the question "What do I see?" In underwater research, the sea frequently covers with sand the very things a person is seeking (only to have it exposed to view months or years later by a storm). A careless searcher might miss the signs and pass over a site, never realizing that what lies below is the very thing he is looking for.

In like manner in our study of the Bible, we need to read the text as if for the first time. We need to project ourselves into what is happening and witness the events as if they were taking place before our eyes (e.g., imagine the lepers finding the Syrian camp deserted [II Kings 7:3-12] or the Apostle Paul chained between Roman soldiers dictating his letters from prison). No detail is trivial or unimportant. And we need patience.

Some years ago, and because our sons were approaching their 20s, my wife and I determined to do something special before their commitments made a vacation together an impossibility. We determined to

---

[3] The importance of accurate *observation, interpretation,* and *application* has been spelled out in detail in the work by H. G. Hendricks and W. D. Hendricks, *Living by the Book* (1991), 349pp. Because they have done such excellent work, what they have written will not be duplicated here. Instead, their principles will be incorporated into our study of the life of Abraham.

cruise the Greek islands of the Mediterranean. And so it was that we spent many happy hours visiting the ruins of old temples and walking through places made famous by events that had transpired there.

I had recently finished reading Lawrence Durrell's *Prospero's Cell*, and told my family one of the stories related by the author. Durrell had been spending a summer on the island of Corfu. Next door to the place where he was staying lived a workman named Anastasius. One night, Durrell became aware of the late hours his neighbor was keeping, for he could hear the sounds of laborious reading.

The next morning Durrell asked Anastasius the reason. With some degree of pride his friend showed him a tattered paper covered book. He then began to explain to Durrell the story (as far as he had progressed) that he had gone to such lengths to read. It was about a warrior named Odysseus who had sailed across the Adriatic to fight at a city named Troy.

Homer's *Odyssey*, which Anastasius had been reading, was one of his young daughter's textbooks. The poor workman had been deprived of an education in his youth and so the fascinating saga of Odysseus' travels reached him fresh and alive as if it had happened yesterday.

Lawrence Durrell then took his excited neighbor for a walk.

"When Odysseus reached here from Fano ...."

"Reached here?" Anastasius asked bewildered.

"Yes, yes," replied Durrell. "Do you know the first of the three bays before the hotel Paleokastrista? It was there that he met the princess. And King Alcinous had his palace under yonder olive trees."

Anastasius' excitement was obvious. The whole narrative had taken on new meaning. Three-thousand-year-old history seemed to have been reborn before his eyes. *And something of that original freshness needs to be recaptured by us in our study of the Bible if God's Word is to become meaningful to us.*

## *Riches for the Taking*

One way we can recreate the reality of the things we read about in the Bible is to think of them happening before our eyes. This involves rethinking the narrative in the present tense. For example, in Acts 7 Stephen describes Abraham's conversion experience. He states that *"the God of glory appeared to our father Abraham when he was in Mesopotamia, before he lived in Haran ..."* (Acts 7:2).

Read over quickly this appears dull, but if you were Abraham how would you describe your experience? From Joshua 24:2-3 we know that Abraham's father was an idolater, and in all probability Abraham himself spent the first seven decades of his life worshipping idols. Then God in all His glory appeared to him. Visualize the scene. What was Abraham's reaction? Could heathen deities offer anything similar? Do you think Abraham ever forgot the experience?

As we begin to sharpen our powers of observation we will need to determine what kind of literature we are reading. Obviously, much of the life of Abraham is *narrative* (Genesis 12-25), but is this all? Other references to Abraham are *poetic* (Psalm 105:1-15); some of it is

# Biblical Investigation 9

*didactic* (Luke 3:8 or 16:19-31); other references to him are *rhetorical* (Matthew 22:31-32) or *dramatic* (Genesis 24:1-9) or *polemical* (Galatians 3:1-22) or even *prophetic* (Genesis 17:1-8)? Each of these comprises a literary form.

We also need to take note of different terms. For example:

**Time** is expressed by words like "after," "now," "when," "as", "then," "while," "before";

**Place** by words like "where," "unto";

**Emphasis** is indicated by "indeed," "only," "behold," "even";

**Reason** by "because," "for," "since";

**Result** by "so," "then," "therefore," "thus";

**Purpose** by "in order that," "so that," "that," and sometimes "to";

**Contrast** by "although," "but," "yet," "otherwise," "nevertheless," "then," "however";

**Comparison** by "also," "and," "as," "like," "so also," "likewise," "similarly," and

**Condition** by "if."

In addition, there is the need to pay attention to the tenses of verbs.[4] As we gain experience, we will develop greater sensitivity to the literary structure and be able to discern the atmosphere of the biblical text. The covenant

---

[4] This is enlarged upon by R. Traina in *Methodical Bible Study* (1985), 34-62.

God made with Abraham (Genesis 15:17-18) will elicit a different response from us than the touching scene when the patriarch went to weep over the body of his dead wife (Genesis 23:2).[5]

In our observation of the text of Scripture, we also need to attune ourselves to clues that are contained in such literary devices as *summary statements* (cf. Genesis 24:1, 35; 25:8); *explanation* (Genesis 21:1); *statements of result* (Genesis 12:5b or 21:2ff.); *cause-and-effect relationships* (Genesis 12:10; 16:1-2, 5); *comparison* or *contrast* (Genesis 12:9-12; 21:8-10; 25:5-6); *repetitious words* or *phrases* (Genesis 17:7-8; 18:22-33; 12:11-13; 20:2, 13: 22:2a; 23:11, 17, 20); *continuation* (Genesis 13:16; 15:5; 18:21); *cruciality* (Genesis 12:14; 15:1; 22:10-12); *a move from the general to the specific* (or vice versa); *explanation* (Genesis 18:16-21); *interrogation* (Genesis 18:9-15); and *chronology* (Genesis 12:4; 16:3; 17:1; 21:5; 23:1; 25:7). All of these will add interest to your study.

## *Importance of the Context*

Those who looked for the *Atocha* knew roughly where to begin their search, but they needed to know as much as they could about the area so that their investigation could be systematic and have a context. The same is true of Bible study. We will be studying the lives of Abraham and

---

[5] And what of Sarah? Was she a "doormat" who lived to do her husband's bidding? In her relationship to him was she like a shadow that followed him around wherever he went? No. Sarah was a powerful woman in her own right. She supervised the entire camp. She entered as best she could into his spiritual experience and did all she could to be lovingly supportive of him (cf. Hebrews 11:8, 11).

Sarah. Abraham is described as *"the father of the faithful"* (Romans 4:16; Galatians 3:7) and Sarah is identified in Scripture as a model wife (I Peter 3:1-6). But where do they fit in the history of the world? What do we know of them and their race? Who were their parents? When were they married? Did they have any children? These are important questions.

For the sake of consistency, we will refer to Abram as Abraham, even though in the early chapters of Genesis we read of Abram, and in like manner we will refer to Sarah as Sarah, though she is first spoken of as Sarai.

It is also vitally important to study a passage of Scripture in its *context*. The Book of Genesis clearly reveals what the biblical writer (Moses) thought was important. For example, two chapters are devoted to Creation and one to the way in which sin entered into the world. This is followed by the recounting of the names of people who lived and died in the millennia that followed (Genesis 4:1-5:32).[6] The next most important event is the Flood. And following the Flood, God instituted civil government (Genesis 6:1-9:29). Next we read of the descendants of Noah (Genesis 10:1-32)—again spanning a considerable period of time—before coming to the Tower of Babel and the dispersal of people over the earth (Genesis 11:1-9). One family is selected, the descendants of Shem, and God's redemptive purpose is now identified with this family. And with that we are introduced to the family of

---

[6] Satan had said to Eve that, if she ate the fruit from the Tree of the Knowledge of Good and Evil, *she would not die.* She did, and so did her posterity. These chapters prove that the devil has been a liar from the beginning (John 8:44).

Abraham (Genesis 11:10-26). After this, the writer devotes fourteen chapters to the life of Abraham, giving him more space than any person or event referred to thus far. It seems evident, therefore, that as interesting as Creation and the Flood are, the writer has passed over millennia in his haste to tell his readers about Abraham.

```
 Creation  Fall  Several Millennia  The Flood  Tower of Babel      Life of Abraham       Jacob/Joseph
 ___,     ___, ............,      ___,      ... ___ ...,    _____,      .........
  1-2      3        4-5            6-9           10            11  -  25            26-50
```

Initially God dealt with the entire human race. The people who lived on the earth, however, showed themselves to be utterly corrupt, and time and again God was compelled to intervene in human history (e.g., at the Flood and at the Tower of Babel) lest Satan thwart His plan of salvation. With Abraham, however, He set aside the nations and chose a man through whom His promise of redemption would be fulfilled (Genesis 3:15).

Can we sense with Moses the importance of the life of Abraham?

## *The Importance of Sensitivity*

I came across a story recently that illustrates the importance of becoming sensitive to the biblical text. It was written by a medical doctor, Richard Selzer.[7] One day

---

[7] *Harper's Magazine* (January 1976), 75-78.

Biblical Investigation 13

as Dr. Selzer was passing the bulletin board of the hospital in which he was working, he saw on a 3"x5" card an announcement: *"Yeshi Dohnden will make rounds at six o'clock on the morning of June 10."* A few particulars as to Dr. Dhonden's eminence as a physician followed.

Not being one to miss such an opportunity, Dr. Selzer joined the clutch of white coats on June 10 and waited for the Tibetan doctor to arrive. At precisely six o'clock, he appeared. He was short, golden skinned, rotund, and dressed in a sleeveless robe of saffron and maroon. He was clean-shaven.

Dr. Dhonden bowed to his colleagues as he entered. He then asked to see the patient who had been selected for the examination. The patient, of course, had been awakened a short time before, advised of what was going to take place, and had been asked to produce a fresh urine specimen.

On entering the room, Yeshi Dhonden noticed the patient's compliance—the attitude of resignation that is frequently expressed by a chronically ill person. He, however, said nothing. Instead, walking quietly to the bed he spent a long time looking at her, yet not so as to cause her embarrassment. No physical sign or obvious symptom gave him a clue as to the nature of her problem. At last, he took her hand in both of his. With his eyes closed he felt her pulse. For what seemed like half an hour, he remained bending over the bed, feeling the evidence of her heart beating and, by unhurried examination, coming to know the state of her health.

Dr. Dhonden's concentration was obvious. He was probing the woman's physical condition and seeking to discover the primary cause of her illness.

At last the Tibetan straightened, gently placed the woman's hand back on the bed and stepped backward. Speaking to his interpreter he asked for a small wooden bowl and two sticks. These were handed to him. He poured a little of the urine into the bowl and proceeded to beat it into froth. Then, bowing over the bowl he slowly inhaled the odor. This done, he set the bowl down and turned to leave.

Before Dr. Dhonden could pass through the door the woman raised her head off the pillow and said, "Thank you, doctor." She evidently felt that in this Asian physician she had found someone who understood her condition and was sensitive to her situation.

Alone with the men of his profession, Yeshi Dhonden gave his diagnosis. Little was lost through the interpreter. He spoke in pictures and symbols as he described winds coursing through the body of an unborn child, and of currents breaking against barriers. Between the chambers of her heart, long before she was born, a "wind" had come up and "blown open a gate" that must never be opened. Through this opening now charged the full waters of her blood stream which "like a mountain stream in springtime cascade downward battering and knocking loose the land."

Without elaborate tests, X-rays, exploratory surgery, or prolonged hospitalization, Dr. Dhonden had diagnosed congenital heart disease, an interventricular septal defect with resultant heart failure.

As Yeshi Dhonden was able to vitally tune in to this woman's body and become intimately aware of her condition, so we should develop an unhurried awareness of what God is saying to us through His Word. It will not happen all at once, but we can develop the skills if we persevere. The process begins with *observation* and an unhurried attempt to read a passage of Scripture in a fresh, intimate and attractive manner.

## INTERACTION

Apply what you have learned from this chapter to the following questions. Write your responses in your notebook so that you can refer to the details quickly and easily.

1. Read carefully Acts 7:2*b*-5. Put yourself in Abraham's position. What was his response to this revelation? Why do you think God separated Abraham from the culture and customs of his times? How would you feel if God told you to leave the place of your birth (or where you are living right now) and go to some obscure region you knew nothing about?

2. What repetitious statements occur in Hebrews 11:8-12? Which two words underlie cause and effect in verse 8? The covenant God made with Abraham is first mentioned in Genesis 12:1-3. It promised Abraham personal, national and universal blessing. Which facet is the subject of Hebrews 11:8-10? Highlight the contrast between Abraham's expectation and his experience.

3. Practice developing sensitivity to Scripture by asking meaningful questions of Acts 7:1-2. Incorporate into your answer information from Joshua 24:2-3.

Chapter Two

# THE IMPORTANCE OF ACCURACY

There is a passage in Lewis Carroll's *Through the Looking Glass* in which he describes Alice's encounter with Humpty Dumpty. Humpty Dumpty was a large egg-like creature with eyes, a nose, and a mouth. As Alice began conversing with him, it appeared that he was ready to argue about anything and everything. And what was so annoying, he assumed he was always right.

At one point, after arguing about birthdays and birthday presents, Humpty Dumpty scoffed at Alice and, as if to show his superiority, said: "There's glory for you!"

"I don't understand what you mean by 'glory,'" Alice said.

Humpty Dumpty smiled contemptuously. "Of course you don't—till I tell you.... When *I* use a word it means just what I choose it to mean—neither more nor less."

To which Alice replied, "The question is whether you *can* make words mean so many different things."[1] And she

---

[1] L. Carroll, *The Annotated Alice* (1960), 268-69.

was right. How can we possibly understand what is being said or written if the meaning is constantly changing?

This quaint story has a bearing on our study of the Bible. The way in which we interpret the words of Scripture is important.[2]

We have all dealt with people who have thrown at us the question, "How can you know that your interpretation is right? Others, including reputable scholars, have looked at the same Scriptures and come away with a different view. Doesn't this prove that the Bible is enigmatic and incomprehensible?"

## SOUND INTERPRETATION

Even evangelicals who believe that the Bible is the inspired word of God sometimes differ over the interpretation of well-known passages. For example, what is your understanding of the story told by the Lord Jesus of the man who went down from Jerusalem to Jericho only to be attacked by thieves who beat him severely and took all of his possessions (see Luke 10:25-37)? What did He intend those who heard Him to glean from what He said? One example of the way this story has been interpreted comes from the famous preacher, Dr. John Gill. Dr. Gill explained the significance of Christ's story this way:

---

[2] A helpful work explaining the principles of interpretation (and including a discussion of different types of literature) is R. B. Zuck's *Basic Bible Interpretation* (1991), 324pp.

## The Importance of Accuracy

This **certain man** may represent mankind fallen in Adam, from a state of happiness into misery ... he may **go down from Jerusalem** (which signifies peace) **to Jericho** (a city accursed by Joshua) and a very wicked city: Since man by sinning against God departed from his happy and perfect state ... and by man **falling among thieves** may be expressed mankind coming into the hands of sin and Satan, which are robbers ... since these have robbed man of his honor, defaced the image of God in him ... [These thieves] **stripped him of his raiment**, signifying the loss of original righteousness ... and wounded him, showing the morbid and diseased condition that sin has brought man into ... **and departed, leaving him half-dead** [i.e., natural death], which comes by sin .... **There came down a certain priest ... and a Levite** ...the priest may represent the moral law, and the Levite the ceremonial; and so both, the whole law of Moses, which intimates that no help may be expected from the Mosaic system.... **But a certain Samaritan** [i.e., Christ], ... **when he saw him** seeing the elect before the fall, came to redeem them. They were by nature the children of wrath, as others, and He washed them from their sins [even as this Samaritan] ... **pouring in oil and wine**: by which, in general, may be designed to represent the blood of Christ applied to the conscience of the wounded sinner ... and **brought him to an inn**, a church of Christ where the gospel guides, directs, and cares for the soul ... **and took care of him**, *clothed him with His righteousness*, fed him with choicest provisions, gave him the reviving cordials of love .... **And on the morrow, when he departed** ... **took two pence** ... which signify, not the law and the gospel, for they [the two denarii] were equal, but as they were given by Christ, seem rather to signify the Old and New Testaments: or as some interpret it, the two sacraments of the Church, baptism and the Lord's Supper ... and **gave them to the inn keeper**; by whom may be meant ministers of the gospel ... to whom has been committed the care and feeding of souls with the words of faith and doctrine....[3]

As creative as Dr. Gill's explanation may be, the real question is, Was this what the Lord Jesus intended to convey to His hearers? Or, put differently, was this what they understood the story to mean? The text clearly states that the occasion of Christ's teaching was in response to the question, *"Who is my neighbor?"* And when the Lord Jesus had finished His story He asked, *"Which of these people [i.e., the priest, the Levite, or the Samaritan] do you think proved to be a neighbor to the man who fell into the hands of robbers?"* The interpretation of the story, therefore, obviously has to do with neighborliness and helping those in need.

The challenge of those who excuse their own ignorance of Scripture by claiming that there are many different (and sometimes conflicting) interpretations of the Bible can be easily answered when we ask, "Which passages do you find confusing or contradictory?" And if we follow carefully the laws of interpretation, we will find

---

[3] J. Gill, *An Exposition of the New Testament* (1809), I:596-97.

that the problems these people deduce are easily resolved. What is important is for us to aim at accurate interpretation and then follow up our investigation with adequate verification. We may not convince all of our critics of our views, but at least *we* will not be *"blown around by every wind of doctrine"* (Ephesians 4:14).

As we begin our study of the Bible we need to have ...

- A regular time for our study of God's Word.
- A regular place for study.
- A regular procedure, and
- A spiral notebook.

## *Principles of Interpretation*

The Christian church has not always followed sound principles of interpretation. From the earliest times many indulged in allegorism. This plunged the church into a quagmire of subjectivity. Perhaps the reason for this may be traced to their desire to have something immediate to nourish their souls. This was not the practice followed by the Lord Jesus and His disciples. The fact is that those who indulged in allegorism ignored the place of observation and interpretation, and moved directly to application. It remained for the reformers—men like John Calvin, Martin Luther, Huldreich Zwingli and John Knox—to bring the church back to a sound system of hermeneutics.[4]

---

[4] F. W. Farrar, in his *History of Interpretation* (1961), 553pp. has given us a readable summary of the different schools of thought.

In spite of the efforts of these godly men, there have always been those who have preferred a spiritual or mystical approach to understanding the Bible. To make the Bible easy to understand, we will follow a three-fold approach involving a *literal, cultural* and *grammatical* approach. As we do so we will find that these steps will keep us from the quicksands of subjectivity.

## *Three Guiding Principles*

First, as interpreters of Scripture we find that the literal approach follows the normal, basic, customary, social designation of the word or phrase. This allows for metaphors and figures of speech that are interpreted in light of the type of literature we are studying (whether poetry or prophecy, parables or typology, history or theology, et cetera). For example, in Christ's parable of the sower and the seed, He illustrated what He wanted to teach His disciples by using the common occurrence of a farmer throwing seed onto a plowed field. His hearers had seen this many times. The literal reality of sowing seed was later explained by the Lord Jesus. The Word of God was like seed that was sown in people's hearts.

The second criterion by which we interpret the Word of God is *cultural*.[5] This involves an awareness of the historic and geographic setting,[6] the manners and customs

---

[5] One of the best works on this subject is Howard F. Vos' *New Illustrated Bible Manners and Customs* (1999), 661pp.

[6] The history of God's people is to be found in L. Wood's *A Survey of Israel's History* (1970), 444pp.; and F. F. Bruce, *New Testament History* (1971), 462pp. The geography of the Bible is found

of the people,[7] the economic and military strengths and weaknesses of the different nations, and their spiritual beliefs and practices.[8] By understanding the cultural background of Ur (located near the Persian Gulf), we know about the society from which Abraham and Sarah came. Then, as we study a map of the region, we can trace their movements all the way from Mesopotamia to Canaan.

The cultural method of Bible study will also equip us with an awareness of what was involved in *"pitching one's tent,"* and enable us to better understand Abraham's association with the Hurrians, Canaanites and Hittites. We will also learn about the agriculture and industry of the different regions; the method of barter; the practice of kings going forth to war; the relation between a suzerain and his vassals; and the socially accepted way of burying one's dead. This will shed light on Abraham's life and times.

Third, and by way of adding precision to the literal and cultural methods already discussed, there is the grammatical interpretation of the text that includes the usage of words, the construction of sentences, and different emphases that are inherent in the original text. All of this sounds intimidating, and for some reminds them of their struggles in seventh grade. Don't be put off. Our approach will not be as technical, and I can promise you it won't be boring!

---

in D. Baly's *The Geography of the Bible* (1974), 288pp., and Y. Aharoni, *The Land and the Book* (1979), 481pp

[7] See Vos' *New Illustrated Manners and Customs* (1999), 661pp

[8] An excellent discussion of the cultural milieu of Abraham's day is contained in John Davis' *Paradise to Prison* (1975), 363pp.

But what is meant by the "original text"? Doesn't that involve a knowledge of Greek and Hebrew and Aramaic?

Those without training in the original languages can make up for what they lack by using a good, accurate translation of the Bible (like the *New American Standard Bible*), and by studying reliable Bible commentaries.[9] And for the encouragement of those who feel they will never be able to succeed in properly interpreting the Bible, let me say that many of the great men and women of the past made up for what they lacked by zealously meditating on the Word and using whatever helps were available to them.

## MARGIN OF PROFIT

The advantages of an accurate interpretation of the Bible are as follows: (1) Our interpretation is grounded in objective, verifiable data; (2) there is adequate control over our interpretation; and (3) this method has historically proved itself in practice. The limitations of this method are that our insistence on accuracy can lead to a dry, pedantic approach to Scripture (II Corinthians 3:6); and depending on our motivation, we may not progress beyond a basic understanding of the text. We must always guard, therefore, against a spirit of pride that comes from "being right" because it may lead to us becoming complacent in regard to God's plan and purpose for His people.

---

[9] See C. J. Barber, *Best Books for Your Bible Study Library* (2000), 96pp. It contains a recommended list of 100+ works ranging from Bible translations, atlases and Bible dictionaries to reliable commentaries on every book of the Bible.

## OFF AND RUNNING

How then may we capitalize on the advantages of proper Bible interpretation and avoid the disadvantages? The answer involves our internal and external selves. Internally, the more the Holy Spirit uses the Word to change our lives, the more humble we should become. This should take care of our susceptibility toward pride. And externally, as we study the Bible to discern the writer's theme, we are caught up in God's progressive revelation of His plan and purpose for mankind.

Many individuals are familiar with select verses from the different books of the Bible, but have never progressed beyond this point to a study of these verses in their context and to the uncovering of the biblical writer's purpose. For example, Genesis is the book of beginnings (of human life, the family, the home, sin, salvation, and human relationships). The book of Ruth is a beautiful story illustrating God's love. The book of Judges shows how, in the worst of times, God's power was available to those who trusted in Him. The books of Samuel deal with the sovereignty of God in His dealings with His people. The book of Nehemiah describes for us the principles of leadership. Song of Solomon is a marital love poem dramatizing the stages and struggles in the relationship of a couple. Jonah has something in it for parents who are bewildered by their teenagers, for it shows how God the Father dealt with His rebellious son. Habakkuk explains how we are to survive when all about us is ready to collapse. Matthew's gospel emphasizes the power of the King and the principles of His Kingdom. John's gospel is a record of the conflict between light and darkness, belief and unbelief. And so we could go on. Sufficient to say that each book of the Bible has a distinct theme or purpose.

How then may we engage in the kind of Bible study that will yield these rewards?

The answer lies in learning how to ask interpretative questions. Rudyard Kipling, in his *Just So Stories*, gave us an important clue. He said,

> I keep six honest serving-men
> (They taught me all I knew):
> Their names are *What* and *Where* and *When*
> And *How* and *Why* and *Who*.

By asking questions of the text we can learn about the *nature* (what), the *place* (where), the *time* (when), the *means* (how), the *purpose* or *reason* (why), and the *people* (who).

This is where the spiral bound notebook comes in. On the left-hand page in the margin, we can place the chapter and verse number, followed by the questions with which we probe each verse. Then on the right hand page, we can write our answers to these questions. It will be found that sometimes we will ask questions of the text that we are unable to answer. This should not cause undue anxiety. Some of the greatest Bible students I know have wrestled for many years with issues that have arisen out of their study of God's Word. Then, when the matter has been almost forgotten, a chance remark or a verse in a seemingly obscure portion of Scripture will flood their minds with new understanding.

Bible study is exciting! We should be patient, therefore, and allow the Bible to speak for itself. It is when we are in a teachable frame of mind (see Isaiah 50:4) that the Holy Spirit can guide us into all truth (I Corinthians 2:14).

## THE BENEFITS OF REFLECTION

The benefits of taking time to understand the text become apparent as we reflect on the process. We find that Scripture becomes profitable for both our creed (i.e., our beliefs) and our conduct. It is profitable because it builds upon the truth. False teachers invariably separate doctrine and experience. As we take a closer look at their teachings, we find that they emphasize the one to the exclusion of the other. The value of knowing the Bible is that it is profitable for doctrine (specifically of the way of salvation, cf. II Timothy 3:15), and for describing our duties. It is valuable for the correction of errors that can so easily corrupt; for the restoration of the one who has fallen; and for training in righteousness. A study of God's Word is also the means God uses to bring a person to maturity (cf. Hebrews 5:13-6:2).

The benefits of a sound interpretation of Scripture are numerous. We will mention only three: (1) Our study is factual; (2) it is also colorful; and (3) in the end it is eminently practical.

It is *factual* in that it is grounded in what God has chosen to reveal. We do not import into our study what someone else has said, no matter how pleasing or plausible it may be. We interpret the Word as it stands and in this way we lay a solid foundation for the application of truth to life. It is *colorful* in that we can recreate the setting in which the events took place. This will give us a new perspective on the lives of those who lived in Bible times. And it is *practical* because we can begin with a single paragraph and progress steadily through an entire book. Such a systematic approach becomes a rewarding experience. Our lives are enriched. We are then able to pass on to others some of the things we have learned.

Of encouragement to us is the psalmist's experience:

*O how I love Your law!*
 *It is my meditation all the day.*
*Your commandments make me wiser than my enemies,*
 *For they are ever mine.*
*I have more insight than all my teachers,*
 *For Your testimonies are my meditation.*
*I understand more than the aged,*
 *Because I have observed Your precepts.*
*I have restrained my feet from every evil way,*
 *That I may keep Your word.*
*I have not turned aside from Your ordinances,*
 *For You Yourself have taught me.*
*How sweet are Your words to my taste!*
 *Yes, sweeter than honey to my mouth!*
*From Your precepts I get understanding;*
 *Therefore I hate every false way.*
                              (Psalm 119:97-104).

## INTERACTION

Read Luke 16:19-31 carefully two or three times. Then, using your notebook, write down interpretative questions on the left hand page (e.g., begin with "Why did the Lord Jesus tell this story?" "Who heard Him?" "What did the Lord Jesus hope His audience would learn?" "Where did the events take place?" "Who was involved?" "Why are the two principal characters contrasted?" etc. Then, on the right hand page, provide as many interpretative answers as you can.

Share your observations with someone.

Chapter Three

# FEAST OF JOY

## THE "HOW-TO" OF APPLICATION

In *Somewhere in Time,* Christopher Reeve plays the part of young writer named Richard Collier who sees a picture of a beautiful actress, Elise McKenna (played by Jane Seymour). He desires more than anything to meet her. There is only one problem: She lived at the turn of the century and may already have died. One of his college professors tells him that if he uses the powers of his mind, he can travel back in time. He decides to do so in order to find the woman of his dreams, and of course, when they meet they fall deeply in love. (What else would you expect in a love story?)[1]

In our study of the Bible we, too, need to travel back in time—not physically, but mentally, for to properly understand the Bible we must know what life was like in Bible times. We must "meet" (in our imagination) the people about whom we read, learn all we can about them, and then bridge the gap between the past and the present so that we can draw parallels between their experiences and our own.

---

1 This story is pure fiction, even though according to the Internet, belief in time travel is still in vogue in some quarters.

But how may this be done? The answer is two-fold: (1) We need to spend time *meditating* on a passage of Scripture until we understand it; and (2) we need to read select books about what life was like in Bible times.

Where the former is concerned we have the example of the late Dr. George Campbell Morgan. He was a school teacher-turned-preacher, and became one of the great Bible expositors of the twentieth century. Lacking a theological education, he determined above everything else to know the Word of God. According to his daughter, Jill, who wrote a biography of her father,[2] as he prepared to preach he would never open a commentary or consult another book until he had saturated his heart and mind with the passage of Scripture to be shared with his congregation. This often took as many as forty or fifty readings of the text. By the time he felt he had a grasp of the portion of the Word to be expounded, he often saw truths in the text (i.e., cause-and-effect relationships, a move from a general statement to identifiable specifics, the subtle use of the imperative, or God's use of means to accomplish His ends, et cetera) that had escaped the notice of many of the finest scholars. It is no wonder that under his preaching, Westminster Chapel in London became one of the great centers of Bible teaching in England.

The principles of Scripture drawn from his careful *observation* and *interpretation* of the text paved the way for his *application* of the Word of God to the lives of those who sat under his ministry.

---

[2] J. Morgan, *Man of the Word* (1951), 404pp. See also J. Harries, *G. Campbell Morgan: The Man and His Ministry* (1930), 252pp.

Second, we can begin reading good books. Only books of significant value should be purchased, and in time each of us can acquire a small but useful library that will adequately support our biblical studies. To begin, you will need a good Bible atlas, an unabridged concordance, and a good Bible dictionary that will help you understand the manners and customs of those living in Bible times. Visit your local Christian bookstore and ask to see *The Moody Atlas of the Bible* by Barry Beitzel, the *New American Standard Bible Concordance* by Robert Thomas, and the *New Unger's Bible Dictionary* by Merrill F. Unger (edited by R. K. Harrison). You do not need to purchase all of these books at one time. Some of them would make an ideal birthday or Christmas present.

## *Turning Point*

As we seek to apply the Scripture to our own situation, we ask the question, *What does this mean to me?* In doing so, we need to remember that while there is only one interpretation of a passage of Scripture, there may be numerous applications. Valid application must, of necessity, be based on accurate interpretation.[3] Take, for example, the Apostle Paul's lengthy discussion of Christian liberty in I Corinthians 8:1-11:1. His principles of proper conduct are set forth within the context of meat offered to idols. Now obviously the dilemma facing first century Christians does not apply to us. Should we do as others

---

[3] See Traina, *Methodical Bible Study*, 214-31.

have done and reject this passage as "culturally conditioned" and of no practical value to us? By no means!

As we read through I Corinthians 8:1-11:1, we obviously interpret what Paul wrote literally, and in doing so gain a better understanding of one of the ethical dilemmas facing those who had so recently been saved from pagan superstition. But the historic context of this passage does not give us license to set it aside as of no value. Latent within these chapters are five principles that should govern our conduct. And these principles are timeless. They may be summarized as follows:

(1) My involvement in something that is ethically permissible may imperil the weak, therefore, my use of liberty should be regulated by love for my weaker brother (I Corinthians 8);

(2) My involvement in something that is ethically permissible may hinder my work for the Lord, therefore I should abstain so that that I can become all things to all men (I Corinthians 9);

(3) My involvement in something that is ethically permissible may endanger my soul, therefore, I should take heed lest I fall (I Corinthians 10:1-13);

(4) My involvement in something that is ethically permissible may identify me with the world, therefore, I should refrain from such activity lest I provoke Christ to jealousy (I Corinthians 10:14-22); and

(5) I should always consider what edifies, and do all things to the glory of God (I Corinthians 10:23-11:1).

Such an approach preserves the literal meaning of Paul's instruction. However, in applying Scripture from a bygone era to our own age, we need to look for *principles*. These principles will be found to transcend social customs, and can easily be applied to those living in Western cultures. Many of these principles of application deal with spiritual realities, ethical standards, social duties, and personal attitudes. As such they apply equally to men and women, for both sexes share the same dynamics of personality and Godward responsibility.

## *Biblical Precedent*

But what of those who remain unconvinced? Can we provide irrefutable justification from the Bible to confirm that this kind of application is valid? When the Apostle Paul wrote to the Christians in Corinth, he said: *"Now these things happened to them [those living in Old Testament times] as an example, and they were written for our instruction, upon whom the ends of the ages have come"* (I Corinthians 10:11).

Let us look at the context (i.e., verses 6-10) to see how the apostle used the Old Testament to illustrate the point he was making.

> *Now these things happened as examples for us, so that we would not crave evil things as they also craved. Do not be idolaters, as some of them were; as it is written, "THE PEOPLE SAT DOWN TO EAT AND DRINK, AND STOOD UP TO PLAY." Nor let us act immorally, as some of them did, and twenty-three thousand fell in one day. Nor let us try the Lord, as some of them did, and were destroyed by the serpents.*

*Nor grumble, as some of them did, and were destroyed by the destroyer.*

These admonitions to right conduct form the basis of Paul's exhortation in verse 11. He then concludes with a warning, *"Now ... let him who thinks he stands take heed that he does not fall"* (I Corinthians 10:12).

The setting of I Corinthians 10:6-10 was the exodus of the Israelites from Egypt. And though the context treats a part of the history of God's people, Israel, yet Paul did not hesitate to *apply* the principles to Gentiles. Why? Because human nature is the same, and there is only one God to whom we are all accountable. This truth is confirmed in Romans 15:4 where we read *"For whatever was written in earlier times was written for our instruction, so that through perseverance and the encouragement of the Scriptures we might have hope."*

But what assurance do we have that the Bible is still relevant today?

A story is told of a woman of nervous temperament who went to see the world-renowned physician of Johns Hopkins University, Dr. Howard A. Kelly. She was a professing Christian and frankly admitted that her anxious state was inconsistent with her beliefs. Instead of receiving the expected tranquilizers, she was told, "The remedy for your trouble is in the Bible. I want you to go home and spend an hour each day reading over and meditating on a passage of Scripture."

" But, doctor," began the bewildered patient.

"Go home and read your Bible for an hour each day," interjected Dr. Kelly firmly, "and in a month come back and see me."

At first the woman was inclined to be angry, but she relented and decided to do as she had been instructed. When she returned to Dr. Kelly a month later, the change was evident.

"I see you have done as I suggested," began Dr. Kelly. "Do you feel that you need any other medication now?"

"No, doctor, I feel like a different person. But how did you know what I needed?"

Taking a well-worn Bible from his desk, Dr. Kelly said, "If I were to omit my daily reading of God's Word, I would not only lose my joy, but I would lose my greatest source of strength and skill." Then he turned to Psalm 119:165 and read, *"Those who love Your law have great peace, and nothing causes them to stumble."*[4]

"That is a truth we all need to remember," he said as he rose to escort her to the door.

## *Delicate Balance*

The problem many of us face is that we don't know how to apply the teaching of the Word to our particular needs. This point was driven home forcefully by two incidents that followed a visit to a dentist. Now visiting a

---

[4] The value of the Bible in helping people has been empirically verified by Paul Meier of the Minirth-Meier Clinics, who wrote of his findings in *Renewing Your Mind in a Secular World* (1985), ch. 2.

dentist has never been one of my favorite pastimes. The occasion of my visit, however, did not concern a minor filling (as unpleasant as that might be), but the removal of two lower impacted wisdom teeth. The operation went as went as well as could be expected, and, looking somewhat like a chipmunk, I decided to stay home from church on Sunday morning. So as not to be accused of being entirely pagan, I positioned myself in front of the TV set and watched a variety of religious programs.

As it happened, the best one came on first. A noted expositor explained the meaning of a particularly difficult passage in Peter's First Epistle. His exegesis was flawless, and the way in which he linked the teaching of the passage with the rest of Scripture was brilliant. His message ended as the choir sang the closing hymn. Yet I felt cheated. Where was the application? What meaning did the passage have for me or any other listener?

The next broadcast service came from a local church. The special effects—fountains, stained-glass windows, choir, majestic pulpit, etc.—were magnificent. The message, however, could as easily have come from a secular "how-to" book. The only time the Bible was referred to was at the beginning when the preacher announced his text. The meaning of Scripture was ignored. What the pastor had to say consisted entirely of "application," but of the worst kind, for it took the form of pious moralizing and a challenge to have a positive mental attitude (as helpful as that can be).

Two hours had now gone by, and I was envying my wife and sons, who were at least fellowshipping with friends and being exhorted from the Word.

## *Learning the Art*

It is in applying biblical truth to life that we frequently experience our greatest difficulty.

It often happens that we are not quite sure how to proceed. Our expectations are high. We want to be able to come up with the same kind of scintillating thoughts found in the writings of our favorite Christian authors. But how do we begin to formulate ideas of our own?

**Be True to Yourself.** First, we need to be honest with ourselves about our spiritual growth. Most of us are not numbered among the spiritual giants of our day. We need, therefore, to be honest in our assessment of our growth and needs, and our application of biblical truth should be based upon needs, interests, problems, or emotional responses that are easily identifiable. As we take a look at the lives of Abraham and Sarah we find it impossible to identify with them leaving Ur for Haran and then Canaan (Genesis 12:1ff.).

Abraham had no sooner settled in Canaan when there was a famine in the land. He chose, therefore, to go to Egypt (Genesis 12:10ff.). He had vast flocks and herds. Most of us do not live on a farm, and so have no firsthand knowledge of the devastation of a drought. And if we want to go anywhere we get in our cars and drive there. How then does the decision of Abraham apply to you and me? The closest we come to a famine is reading about droughts or floods or winter's frost in our daily newspapers. And our only source of concern is the rising food prices at the supermarket. Furthermore, most of us live in an industrial and informational environment far removed from the unique pressures of an agrarian economy.

On careful examination, however, we find that Abraham was motivated to go to Egypt because of *fear* (Genesis 20:13*a*). His fear arose from his feeling of aloneness. He had no extended family to help him in a time of crisis. We can begin to apply his situation to our own lives when we identify the famine as an *external threat* compounded by an absence of aid from our family. Now we all know what external threats are like. A bad economic situation (i.e., a recession) may cause monetary resources that have been promised to us for research and development to dry up or be diverted elsewhere. A reversal of policy may result in plans that were particularly dear to us being postponed or canceled. A hike in the price of oil causes an escalation in the cost of gasoline and heating oil to go up. If our companies begin "down sizing" we become fearful lest we suddenly find ourselves without a job. In addition, an unexpected illness may siphon off our funds and leave us with insufficient resources for a comfortable retirement. And so we could go on.

These and other external threats give us greater empathy for Abraham and Sarah. For Abraham's part, instead of waiting for a bad situation to become worse (i.e., for his precarious economic position to deteriorate still further), he decided to do something about it. He tackled the problem before it became a predicament. And with this reasoning we have established a principle that we can apply to a variety of situations.

With a workable principle it becomes much easier for us to apply biblical truth to life. This is done on the basis of identifiable (i.e., parallel) experiences and/or emotional responses. And with a clearly identified principle it becomes a relatively simple matter for us to apply the teaching of the text.

By way of summary, therefore, as we apply the truth of the Bible to our lives, we look for principles that find a parallel in needs, interests, problems, or emotional experiences. But there is a need for us to be brutally honest with ourselves. We may not see the things that Pastor Wise sees because we lack his experience, and we may not be able to apply the truth in quite the same manner as Dr. Blank because we lack his knowledge. But with perseverance and a reliance on the Holy Spirit we will be able to derive life-enriching insights from our study of the Word.

**Be True to the Teaching of the Word.** Second, our application must be in harmony with the teaching of the rest of Scripture. Because God is the Author of all truth, at no time will the teaching of one part of Scripture differ from or be in conflict with what is taught elsewhere in the Bible. In other words, truth in one area will always be consistent with truth in another area of Scripture. This provides a secure basis for our application of the teaching of Scripture to our needs.

In Abraham's experience, as he and Sarah went down to Egypt, he persuaded her to collaborate with him in a deliberate plan of deception. (We will discuss his strategy later on.) Because Sarah was his half-sister did not make his deception acceptable or even permissible. It remained a lie. Years later, when he would attempt to rationalize the situation (see Genesis 20:8-13), his explanation would be shown to have as much substance as a rotten log.

Let us remember, therefore, that when applying Scripture to life, we need to exercise care and not read into the Bible more than is actually there. If we err in this respect, then what we do will not agree with the teaching of other portions of God's Word. The more we know of the Bible, the less likely we will be to reach conclusions that are out of harmony with God's overall revelation.

**Be Committed to Your Own Spiritual Growth.** Third, in the application of biblical truth, we need to keep in mind the needs of our entire being—intellectual, emotional, relational, volitional, and spiritual. Many modern psychologists find that their counseling is more successful when they work with a person's emotions. Pastors, too, have learned that by making their congregations feel guilty (for guilt is a powerful emotion), they can motivate them to give toward the building fund or to missions or to engage in a visitation program. The Bible, however, continually stresses the mind as the place where the process of change begins (see Ephesians 4:23; Colossians 3:10). Consider the Apostle Paul's words in Romans 12:2: *"Do not be conformed to this world, but be transformed by the renewing of your mind, so that you may prove what the will of God is, namely, that which is good and acceptable and perfect [or mature]."*

In applying the truth of the Word to our lives, we need to challenge our thought processes with the desirability of a course of action. This will give our minds the opportunity to give input to our emotions. When our minds and our emotions are working in harmony (i.e., congruently), they will give balanced direction to our wills. The result will be experiential change of lasting duration.

# Feast of Joy

By building on our interpretative questions and answers (as explained in our last chapter), we come to see how we may take each question one step further and use it as a springboard to a valid application of the Bible to our own lives and situations. Once we have identified a basic emotion or dilemma (e.g., like an external threat), we can begin to apply the rest of the text to ourselves, our families, our relatives, our close friends, and our work, et cetera.

Our application of the text, therefore, should be in terms of *principles*. It should also be personal, honest, and mind-expanding. The result will be growth in all areas of life.[5]

## CORRELATION

One step remains. It is *correlation*—the bringing of different truths together so that we are able to develop a sound biblical approach to life. In this stage we ask and answer the question, *How does this contribute to a balanced view of life?*

Dr. Robert Traina defines the process in the following way:

> The goal of Scriptural study is the development of a vital biblical theology issuing in a vital Christian philosophy of life. In order to accomplish this, one must do more than examine individual

---

[5] For an edifying example of this approach, see W. H. Griffith Thomas' *Genesis, a Devotional Commentary* (1946), 112-222.

passages. One must coordinate one's findings so as to evolve a synthesized concept of the message of the Bible. And having done this, one must attempt to relate it to those facts that one discovers outside the Scriptures.[6]

One way we can begin to correlate the teaching of Scripture into a life-view is to define the different areas in which we are called upon to function. We must begin, of course, with the basic prerequisite—(we must be Christians.) This means that at some time in the past, in a personal way, we came into a vital and personal relationship with Jesus Christ. We must know that, on the basis of His sacrifice of Himself for us (which theologians call "the atonement"), our sins have been forgiven and we have been saved from the penalty that our transgressions so justly deserve. As those who now belong to Christ (i.e., as Christ's ones), the first area of our lives to be impacted by the process of correlation is spiritual growth (Ephesians 4:15; Colossians 2:6-7; I Peter 2:2; and II Peter 3:18). We daily require nourishment to sustain our bodies, and our spirits require nourishment too.

Other areas of application (where the teaching of Scripture can be correlated into a doctrinal framework) include the principles that govern our social relationships. This can be described in terms of concentric circles. It begins with the inner circle of husband/wife and then parent/child; this is then enlarged or expanded to include Christian relatives as well as Christian friends; then unsaved relatives on both sides of the family; then unsaved friends and acquaintances. Within a wider scope, there is

---

[6] Traina, *Methodical Bible Study*, 223.

our work and the influence we may have on our colleagues. The more we follow the teaching of God's inspired revelation, the more it will change our attitude toward our jobs, our employer, and those with whom we work (Colossians 3:23). Then, as the circle widens, there is the area of our social and civic life.[7] God made us social beings. How then does the teaching of His Word regulate our choice of friends, entertainment, and recreation?

As a result of searching the Scriptures, we learn how to avoid the extremes of legalism on the one hand and license on the other. This results in a life that demonstrates the enjoyment of liberty. And when it comes to the local assembly of which we are a part, we can serve the church without being dependent on it for spiritual growth.

All of these areas—and others which you can add because they are part of your experience (e.g., military service, professional associations, unions, etc.)—are ones in which you can demonstrate growth. One final point needs to be borne in mind: *Correlation is a lifelong process.* For this reason many people give up. They then wander aimlessly through life, unstable, unsure of themselves, and unable to provide cogent answers for their beliefs. True correlation is vitally related to the integration of faith and experience. It does not pride itself on its accomplishments, nor is it dogmatic. It does give evidence of a powerful inner dynamic that is seen in the commitment to seek out and know (experientially) the truth.

---

[7] See the excellent book by R. D. Culver, *Toward a Biblical View of Civil Government* (1974), 308pp.

As a result of the correlation of biblical truth with life, we can walk in wisdom toward the unsaved, so that they will not be able to criticize our behavior or our doctrine (Colossians 4:5). We will also be able to think clearly (John 8:32; Matthew 6:22-23), probe the essence of different issues (I Corinthians 2:15-16), and have a correct estimate of our selves (Philippians 2:3-11). We will also be Christ-centered (Colossians 3:17) rather than self-centered. And being freed from self-seeking we will be able to focus on others (I Corinthians 10:24; Galatians 6:10). The result of this freedom will be seen in our happiness and genuine fulfillment. We will enjoy peace in the midst of the tensions, pressures, and anxieties of daily living, and with the Apostle Paul we will find that this life is a continuous pageant of triumph in Christ (II Corinthians 2:14-3:6).[8] Above all, we will give evidence of the fruit of the Holy Spirit in our life (Galatians 5:22-23).

With these four techniques: *Observation* (What do I see?), *Interpretation* (What does it mean?), *Application* (What does it mean to me?), and *Correlation* (How does this contribute to a biblical approach to life?) we are ready to engage in the exciting study of what God has chosen to reveal to us!

---

[8] See the remarkable book by Ray C. Stedman, *Authentic Christianity* (1975), 37-77.

## INTERACTION

Practice what you have read in this chapter on Genesis 18. Probe the text by asking questions beginning with "what" followed by "why," "when," "where," "how," and "who." Write down your questions in your spiral notebook, and then attempt to provide answers.

As you progress, ask yourself, "How does the teaching of these verses impact my life?"

Later on, you can expand your questioning to include your spouse, children, relatives and friends, job, and community.

Even if this takes a week, persevere with the process. When you have finished, share your insights with your spouse or a friend.

Chapter Four

# ON THE RIGHT TRACK

## THE SYNOPTIC METHOD

Each summer American families take to the road for their annual vacation. After the luggage has been loaded into the car, SUV or van, and with nothing more than a foldout road map and a tank of gas, the family is off to visit relatives or some of the scenic places of interest in different states. None would dare undertake such a journey without a map, and the more time spent studying it the fewer times one of our children will inform us, "We're lost."

### *Looking Ahead*

The synoptic method of Bible study is like the road map. It enables us to do with a passage of Scripture what families do when they go on vacation. As we chart a portion of Scripture, we gain a better understanding of where we're going. But how is this done? One of the easiest ways is with a chart.

Charts fall into two separate groups. Dr. Robert Traina in his excellent book, *Methodical Bible Study*, describes them as follows:

Charts may be classified in two categories: *horizontal* charts and *vertical* charts. There are variations of both of these, but they represent the main types of charts. The former is used in passages where the perspective is important, such as larger units of material; the latter is frequently helpful in the study of shorter units, such as segments.

*Making charts is easy.* All you need is a pencil, ruler, notebook, and perhaps some Scotch tape in case you need to join two or more pages together. Begin by drawing a horizontal line. Next mark off the number of paragraphs in the section to be surveyed. One column will be allocated for each paragraph. For our purposes we will also assume that each new chapter begins a new paragraph.

If we are studying the life of Isaac (Genesis 25:19-27:46), we draw our chart as follows:

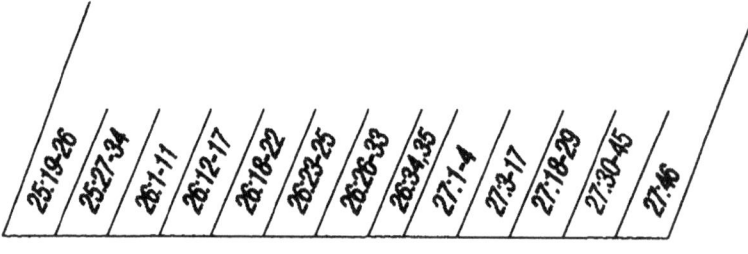

*Chart #1*

Our next task is to give each paragraph a title in keeping with its content. This helps us do several things:

- It helps us see the whole as well as the parts.
- It helps us put into practice the principles of *observation* discussed in chapter 1, noting cause and effect relationships, how the writer works

toward a climax, repetitious statements, proportion (i.e., how much space is devoted to certain topics, and, by contrast, how little is given to others),[1] special points of emphasis, summation, etc.

- It helps us see at a glance the sequence of events in the story.
- It helps us ascertain how all of this contributes to the biblical writer's theme.

*Dos and Don'ts*

Here are a few specifics that will prove helpful.

- Keep the chart clear and simple.
- Focus on the structure of the book,[2] or a person's life,[3] or the history of the period,[4] or a specific subject matter,[5] as the case may be.

---

[1] For example, in studying the life of Jephthah (Judges11-12), note how much space is devoted to redressing the wrongs done Jephthah and how little space is devoted to the actual battle (Judges 11:32-33).

[2] For example, the structure of the Book of Daniel is by language. Chapters 1:1-2:4*a* are in Hebrew, chapters 2:4*b*-7:28 are in Aramaic, and chapters 8:1-12:13*a* are in Hebrew. This dictates clearly what part of God's message was for His people, Israel, and what part was for Gentiles.

[3] The life of Moses was divided into three periods of forty years each (cf. 40 years as prince of Egypt, then 40 years shepherding

- Take into account specific words or phrases (e.g., Habakkuk 2:4 that is repeated three times in the New Testament [Romans 1:17; Galatians 3:11; and Hebrews 10:38]).
- Note how the book begins and ends. What has happened in between?[6]

In general, we should *not* try to put everything onto one chart. It is better to make more than one chart than to put too much on to a single chart. Instead, concentrate on the dominant ideas. Then give each paragraph a title. Determine which paragraphs deal with a similar subject matter or show the progress of an idea. These should be grouped together. If certain paragraphs do share a common subject matter, they can be given a title. Lastly, we should give a title to the entire chart—one that aptly describes its main theme or emphasis.

Your chart of Isaac's life might look something like this:

---

the sheep of his father-in-law, then 40 years leading the Israelites through the wilderness. See Acts 7:30, 36; Hebrews 3:17; and Deuteronomy 34:7).

[4] Cf. Haggai's prophecy that was given at four specific times on three specific days. Noting this (with the exact day indicated in each instance) provides a clue to the divisions of the book.

[5] The Apostle Paul's treatment of Christology in Colossians.

[6] Cf. I Samuel that begins with the birth of Samuel and ends with the death of King Saul. What had happened between these events? The monarchy had been instituted.

# On the Right Track

## THE TRIALS OF ISAAC'S LIFE

| | DOMESTIC TENSIONS | | | | ECONOMIC HARDSHIPS | | | | | DOMESTIC TRIALS | | |
|---|---|---|---|---|---|---|---|---|---|---|---|---|
| | Day in birth of Isaac's sons | Differing outlook of Isaac's sons | Isaac's deception about Rebekah | Blessing in the face of rejection | Frustration met by patience | Return home met with approval | Divine reversal of Philistine rejection | Esau, the beggar, live examples | Isaac desires to bless Esau | Rebekah's plan to secure the blessing for Jacob | Jacob deceives his father | Esau's anger at being cheated | Rebekah's plan to save Jacob's life |
| | 25:19-26 | 25:27-34 | 26:1-11 | 26:12-17 | 26:18-22 | 26:23-25 | 26:26-33 | 26:34,35 | 27:1-4 | 27:5-17 | 27:18-39 | 27:40-41 | 27:46 |
| Godward Orientation | Isaac 21 Rebekah 22 | (Esau none) | | | | Isaac 25 | | Esau None | Isaac fails | Rebekah Shows None | Jacob None | | |
| Covenant | | | 3-5 | | See Gen. 12:3 | Returns to land | | | | | 27-29 | | |
| Personalities | Isaac Rebekah | Jacob Esau | Isaac Abimelech | | | | Isaac Abimelech | Esau | Isaac Esau | Rebekah Jacob | Isaac Jacob | Isaac Esau | Rebekah |
| Emotions | | Esau Impatient Jacob guileful | Fear 2-6 | Envy | Hostile opposition | | Fear 29 | Note Esau's actions | Sensual indulgence | Rebekah Isaac fear | | | |
| Lessons | | | Isaac endures Rebekah's Ostracism | Isaac forbearance | Isaac discerning | | Former Wrongs righted | | | No loving Confrontation or discussion | | | |

Remember that at this stage of your investigation everything is tentative. Allow yourself the liberty of changing the wording, the grouping together of material, and the assigning of a title. Furthermore, spare yourself endless hours of frustration in trying to provide alliterative headings, and in this way avoid the common error of trying to force Scripture into an alliterative mold.

Finally, by extending your chart with horizontal lines and vertical lines (as shown above) you can create rectangular boxes in which to note recurring topics worthy of further study. The verse and/or verses that mention the topic, or a brief descriptive statement, will serve to remind you of what you deemed to be important at the time you constructed your chart.

Don't become discouraged if your first efforts seem to be less than "professional" or if they do not measure up to your ideals. Keep on trying. Rework your chart as you see fit. In time you will enjoy immeasurably the fruits of this method of Bible study. You will also be amazed at how much you have learned!

In the course of your study of the life of Abraham you will make a chart of Genesis 12:1-25:11. Remember that this approach to a portion of Scripture seeks to see specific sections of the book as a unit. At this stage you are not concerned with the fine details. Later on, after the broad movements have been mastered, you will be able to begin analyzing the parts.

## *Plan for Enrichment*

Here are a few suggestions that will enrich your study:

(1) Search for clues as to what was uppermost in the mind of the writer (i.e., his theme, the purpose of his writing; cf. John 20:30-31);

(2) Observe his logic as he develops his theme. Ask interpretative questions and seek to secure interpretative answers;

(3) Note in the rectangular boxes areas of application;

(4) Then ask yourself, "Where else in Scripture is this material treated? How does what is recounted here relate to what is recorded there?"

## THE ANALYTICAL METHOD

A road map is indispensable to the success of our summer vacation. After all, we do want to get to the place(s) we've chosen to visit. However, when entering a city to spend the night or to find a friend's home, we need something with a little more detail.

When it comes to a study of the Bible, the extra detail corresponds to an analysis of the text.

Before I describe the process of analysis, let me share with you a story. When my wife and sons and I lived in Buffalo Grove, Illinois, I frequently took the family to the shores of Lake Michigan on Sunday afternoons. We all enjoyed the outing, and the drive from our home through the well-wooded suburbs provided a constant change of scenery as the trees and shrubs kept pace with the different seasons.

Near our home was a bonsai garden. In this world of diminutive trees and shrubs, the Japanese owners carried on the ancient art of bonsai. By carefully potting seedlings and periodically pruning away their roots, they were able to restrict each plant's growth.

One Sunday as we were returning from the lake, I turned into this bonsai garden. As we walked up and down the carefully manicured paths, we saw eighty-year-old trees, gnarled and weather-beaten, yet standing only thirty inches high. Their potential for growth had been taken from them by the removal of most of their roots.

As beautiful as the art of bonsai may be in the natural world, it is tragic in the spiritual realm, for Christians, with all the opportunities for growth that are available to them, may nevertheless be dwarfed in stature because they have never rooted themselves deeply in the Word of God (cf. Colossians 2:7). Spiritual growth is important. One way to insure that we become "rooted and grounded" in the truth is through a systematic analysis of the passages of the Bible we are studying.

The late Dr. Merrill C. Tenney described the process as follows:

> The analytical method [of Bible study] consists of three distinct stages: the mechanical layout, which involves rewriting the text in a form that will reveal the grammatical structure; the formulation of an outline which will show by reasoning back from the grammatical structure to the meaning how the thoughts of the text are related to each other; and the recording of personal observations on the text as thus analyzed, in order

to find both the explicit and the implicit truths it contains.[7]

Bible analysis is essential whenever we are studying the Epistles or some doctrinal portion of Scripture, for it is the only way to follow the biblical writer's thought, recognize his digressions, and be able to trace the unfolding of his theme. But at the thought of a literary analysis being involved in Bible study, some recoil as they remember what they went through in the seventh grade. And with such a painful reminder of the past, they are prepared to put aside their pencils and opt for remaining spiritual pigmies for the rest of their lives. Such despair is not necessary. No one is going to grade you on your work. The procedure for analyzing the text is quite simple. We will take a look at a couple of examples.

The analytical method proceeds paragraph by paragraph, with the intent of opening up the biblical writer's theme. Initially we look for the verb or verbs in the paragraph. Then we take note of the way in which subordinate sentences and/or clauses are grouped around them. The purpose of a grammatical diagram is to lay bare the real message of the passage. Each line in our diagram will contain one main statement and its modifiers. Subordinate clauses and phrases are indented above and below the lines of the main statement, depending on whether they precede or follow it in order of the text.

We will illustrate these principles with two examples, the first of which will be from the Epistle of Jude (1:20-21),

---

[7] M. C. Tenney, *Galatians: The Charter of Christian Liberty* (1954), 165.

and the second from the Book of Nehemiah. As we begin to develop our analytic skills, we come face to face with a matter of great importance. It concerns which version or translation of the Bible to use. An accurate translation is a must! To illustrate the importance of this point, let us take a look at Jude 1:20-21 in a variety of different translations. The text of each is printed below for convenience.

**King James Version (KJV)**
*"But ye, beloved, building up yourselves on your most holy faith,praying in the Holy Ghost, keep yourselves in the love of God, looking for the mercy of our Lord Jesus Christ unto eternal life."*

**Revised Standard Version (RSV)**
*"But you, beloved, build yourselves up in your most holy faith; pray in the Holy Spirit; keep yourselves in the love of God; wait for the mercy of our Lord Jesus Christ unto eternal life."*

**New International Version (NIV)**
*"But you, dear friends, build yourselves up in your most holy faith and pray in the Holy Spirit. Keep yourselves in God's love as you wait for the mercy of our Lord Jesus Christ to bring you to eternal life."*

**New King James Version (NKJV)**
*"But you, beloved, building yourselves up on your most holy faith, praying in the Holy Spirit, keep yourselves in the love of God, looking for the mercy of our Lord Jesus Christ unto eternal life."*

### New American Standard Bible (NASB)
*"But you, beloved, building yourselves up on your most holy faith, praying in the Holy Spirit, keep yourselves in the love of God, waiting anxiously for the mercy of our Lord Jesus Christ to eternal life."*

In identifying the main statements, we naturally look for the verbs. Underline the verbs in each of the above translations. The *RSV* and *NIV* have four verbs: "build, pray, keep, and wait." What could be simpler? Why then do the others have only one verb, "keep"?

The interesting point is that the Greek text contains only one verb: Keep! The other three statements are participial and should be translated *"building yourselves up . . . praying in the Holy Spirit . . . waiting for the mercy of our Lord Jesus Christ."*

So how can we know which version is right? This is where a Greek Interlinear New Testament can be most helpful. The following contains the Greek text on the first line with a literal translation underneath.

Humeís dé agapeetoí epoikodomoúntes
you, But beloved, building up

heautoús teé hagiootátee humoón pístei
yourselves most holy on your faith,

en Pneúmati Hagíoo proseuchómenoi
in Spirit, (the) Holy praying

```
heautoús      en       agápee        Theoú
yourselves in (the)    love          of God,

teereésate prosdechóminoi tó   éleos toú
Keep       looking for    the mercy of

kuríou heemoón Ieesoú Christoú eis
Lord   of our  Jesus  Christ   unto

zooeén aioónion.
life   eternal.
```

First, locate and underline the main verb. Then take note of the participles. They are clearly identifiable. But why is accuracy so important? Because it underlies certainty. By establishing our faith upon the accuracy of what God has revealed, we have confidence that what we believe is indeed the truth.

Let us take this a step further. In the quotation from Dr. Tenney's book, we found that the first step is to make a mechanical layout of the text, then to formulate an outline, and finally to record our observations. In formulating a mechanical layout, statements that begin at the extreme left-hand side of the page are ones that contain main verbs; modifiers are indented and become subpoints. In taking the NASB text of Jude 1:20-21 our analytical outline would look something like this.

"*But you, beloved*
    A. *Building yourselves up on your most holy faith*
    B. *Praying in the Holy Spirit*

***Keep yourselves in the love of God***
  *C. Waiting anxiously for the mercy of our Lord Jesus Christ."*

Our next step is for us to formulate an outline based on our grammatical structure. What heading might we give Jude's closing exhortation? He is obviously (in this part of his letter) admonishing Christians. We might wish, therefore, to tentatively assign the following heading:

*Jude's Final Admonition in Light of the Times*

Our outline would look something like this:

A. The Specific Requirement
   Keep yourselves in the love of God.
B. The Method to Be Used
   1. Outwardly, by building ourselves up
   2. Inwardly, by praying in the Holy Spirit
C. The Result to Be Expected
   Waiting anxiously for the mercy of our Lord Jesus Christ (at His coming).

But we are not finished. We now need to record our reflections on what we have just done. Let's see what Dr. Alexander MacLaren said about this sentence:

> Jude has been, in all the former part of the letter, pouring out a fiery torrent of vehement indignation and denunciation against *"certain men"* who had *"crept"* into the Church, and were SPREADING GROSS IMMORALITY THERE. He does not speak of them so much as heretics in

belief, but rather as evildoers in practice; and after the thunderings and lightning, he turns from them with a kind of sigh of relief and an emphatic, *"But ye! beloved."* The storm ends in the gentle rain; and he tells the brethren who are yet faithful how they are to conduct themselves in the presence of prevalent corruption, as well as the source of their security and their peace.

You will observe that in my text there is embedded, in the middle of it, a direct precept: *"Keep yourselves in the love of God";* and that is encircled by three clauses, like each other in structure, and unlike it—*"building," "praying," "looking."* ... Why did Jude put two of these similar clauses in front of his direct precept, and one of them behind? I think that because the two that preceded indicate the ways by which the precept is kept, and the one that follows indicates the accompaniment or issue of obedience to the precept.[8]

If we had followed the four main clauses of either the RSV or NIV we would not have known exactly *how* God expects us to keep ourselves in His love in the midst of all that is going on about us, and we would not have understood clearly the outcome of our obedience.

The notes, which Dr. Tenney recommends that we make, are of a personal nature and are derived from our reflection on the text. I included a passage from the pen of

---

[8] A. Maclaren, *Expositions of Holy Scripture*, XVII:97.

Alexander MacLaren to give you some idea of the kind of information that can be gleaned from a single sentence.

## *Patriarchal Example*

Now let us consider another passage, this time an entire paragraph, Nehemiah 9:5-8. It is complete with introductory statement, main theme, and subordinate clauses:

> *Then the Levites, Jeshua, Kadmiel, Bani, Hashabneiah, Sherebiah, Hodiah, Shebaniah and Pethahiah, said, "Arise, bless the LORD your God forever and ever! O may Your glorious name be blessed and exalted above all blessing and praise! You alone are the LORD. You have made the heavens, the heaven of heavens with all their host, the earth and all that is on it, the seas and all that is in them. You give life to all of them and the heavenly host bows down before You. You are the LORD God, who chose Abram and brought him out from Ur of the Chaldees, and gave him the name Abraham. You found his heart faithful before You, and made a covenant with him to give him the land of the Canaanite, of the Hittite and the Amorite, of the Perizzite, the Jebusite and the Girgashite—to give it to his descendants. And You have fulfilled Your promise, for You are righteous.*

The outline of these verses must be developed within the larger context of the whole prayer. It is a prayer in which God's grace is exalted and man's sin is exposed. However, even in this paragraph we see the adoration, praise, and worship which should always characterize true petitioners (Philippians 4:6; Colossians 2:7; 4:2; I Thessalonians 5:18).[9] We also note that when God's greatness and power are brought to mind, He becomes greater and problems are reduced to size.

In verse 7 God's grace is further manifested in His sovereign choice of Abraham. The mention of the covenant that He made with him immediately recalls the *national*, *personal*, and *universal* blessings that are an integral part of this covenant.

Finally, the Levites link themselves and those in Jerusalem who had returned from captivity to the Abrahamic Covenant, and they thank God for fulfilling His promise.

In this context, then, we may proceed with our analysis of these verses and then outline their content.

v.5 Then the Levites ... said
    Jeshua,
    Kadmiel,
    Bani,
    Hashabneiah,
    Sherebiah,
    Hodiah,
    Shebaniah and
    Pethahiah
"Arise, bless the LORD you God forever and ever!
    O may Your glorious name be blessed
        and
        exalted above all blessing and praise!

v.6 "You alone are the LORD.
    You have made the heavens,
        the heaven of heavens with all their host,
        the earth and all that is on it,

---

[9] See the author's book *Nehemiah and the Dynamics of Effective Leadership* (1976), 130-32.

> the seas and all that is in them,
> You give life to all of them, and
> the heavenly host bows down before You.

v. 7-8 "You ... chose Abram, and
> brought him out from Ur of the Chaldess,
> gave him the name Abraham.
> And You found his heart faithful before You
> Made a covenant with him
> to give him the land of the Canaanite,
> Hittite
> Amorite
> Perizzite
> Jebusite
> Girgashite-
> to give to his descendants.

"And You have fulfilled Your promise, for You are righteous."

This mechanical layout may be formed into an outline as follows:

*The Prayer of the Levites*

Introduction: The Leadership of the Levites (Neh. 9:5*a*)

I. The Call to Worship (9:5-8)[10]
    A. The Glory of the One Worshipped (9:5*b*)
    B. The Uniqueness of the One Worshipped (9:6*a*)

---

[10] Roman numeral II would naturally be assigned to the next paragraph.

C. The Power of the One Worshipped (9:6b)
      1. In the heavens
      2. In the inner sanctuary of heaven
      3. On the earth
      4. In the sea
      5. Conclusion
         (a) He is the Source of life
         (b) He has the right to be worshipped.
   D. The Sovereignty of the One Worshipped (9:7-8a)
      1. His Choice of Abraham
      2. His Guidance of Abraham
      3. His Purpose for Abraham
         (a) The faithfulness God found in Abraham
         (b) The covenant God made with Abraham
            (1) The land God gave to Abraham
            (2) The land God gave to Abraham's descendants
   E. The Faithfulness of the One Worshipped (9:8b)

## *Long-Range Gains*

So far in this chapter we have considered how to make charts and the benefits of the analytical method of Bible study. The former focused attention on a single sentence (Jude 1:20-21) whereas the latter concentrated on a paragraph (Nehemiah 9:5-8).

We may now ask ourselves, What are the values of this method of Bible study? Are there any special benefits to be derived from an analysis of the text?

- The analytical method enables us to probe the text in such a way that our finite minds can grasp the riches of God's plan and purpose for us. It lays bare the essential truth of a passage in a way that other approaches do not.
- Our study becomes personal. We are not trafficking in secondhand truths. Our involvement is optimal. We need to probe incisively the literary mold in which God's truth is contained in order to be able accurately to analyze the text.
- This process makes the application of biblical truth easy to appropriate. The central teaching is clearly established in our minds. We also have a greater understanding of the reason for the supporting data.
- The whole process enables us to saturate our minds with God's Word and think His thoughts. In the time we spend exposing ourselves to what He has chosen to reveal to us, we find that our values are being challenged and our beliefs strengthened.
- This approach to Bible study produces spiritual growth more speedily than any other method.

Personally, I find this method invaluable. It has been my desire, whenever I have been studying Paul's letters, to do an analysis of a paragraph each day. I know that this is not very much and that other people may have the time to do much more. However, in connection with my other studies of Scripture, I try to develop a mechanical layout for a small section and then study it as incisively as possible. While writing this book I have been working my way through Paul's letter to the Colossians. I find that when this procedure is followed, commentators can be consulted with greater profit.

The analytic method of Bible study also reminds me of the exhortation of the Apostle Paul: *"As you therefore have received Christ Jesus the Lord, so walk in Him, having been firmly rooted and now being built up in Him and established in your faith, just as you were instructed, and overflowing with gratitude"* (Colossians 2:6-7). You do not have to be a "bonsai" Christian; you can grow into a strong cedar tree.

The psalmist David also spoke eloquently of the blessings received by the diligent Bible student. In Psalm 1:1-3 he portrayed the results to the person who delights in God's "law" (i.e., God's Word). His language is picturesque.

> *O the bliss of the man who does not walk in the counsel of the wicked, nor stand in the path of sinners, nor sit in the seat of scoffers! But his delight is in the law of the LORD, and in His law he meditates day and night. He will be like a tree firmly planted by streams of water that yields its fruit in its season, and its leaf does not wither; and in whatever he does, he prospers.*

The *"delights"* that await us are obvious. Here are a few guidelines to help you persevere until you have mastered the art of analyzing short portions of Scripture. Only then need you move on to extended passages. In the process you will experience growth as your spiritual roots penetrate deeply into the soil of God's Word. You will also begin to find that your understanding of Scripture will help you face the vicissitudes of life (see Psalm 119:165). And you will be able to discern the error inherent in false teaching and become stable in your faith, so that you will not be *"swayed about by every wind of doctrine."* Above all, you will be able to enjoy fellowship with each Member of the Godhead in a way you have never experienced before.

## INTERACTION

Begin your own analysis of Scripture by focusing your attention on Genesis 12:1-3. Read these verses over several times, noting repetitious statements, the use of connectives, cause-and-effect relationships, movement from the general (e.g., *"country"*) to the specific (e.g., *"father's house"*), the parallelism between becoming a *"great nation"* and Abraham's name becoming great, the close connection between obedience and blessing, the promise of protection, and the anticipation for Abraham (and for his descendants) of worldwide influence.

Chapter Five

# LOVE LETTERS

## THE GEOGRAPHIC METHOD

Soren Kierkegaard, the Danish existential philosopher, was a prolific writer. In his essay, "The Mirror of the Word" (based on James 1:22-25), he described the attitude that all believers should have toward Scripture. To make his point plain, he relates a story about a young man who receives a letter from his sweetheart. How does he read it?

In private, with bated breath, absorbing the contents, weighing each thought and expression. Why? The letter is important to him. It is the latest disclosure of the one whom he loves. The application is clear. As precious as this letter is to the lover, just so precious to you, I assume, is God's Word; in the way the lover reads this letter, just so, I assume, do you read God's Word.[1]

Kierkegaard's point is well taken. His emphasis is clear. His analogy, however, needs modification. The Bible is the disclosure of the will of *a loving Father to the child whom He loves.* It is vitally important, therefore, that we do not neglect what He has seen fit to communicate to us.

---

[1] S. Kierkegaard, *Self-Examination* (1946), 51.

## The Call of Abraham

Our first thought as we consider Genesis 12:1-3 is the covenant God made with Abraham. In a sovereign way, the *"Lord of glory"* appeared to Abraham in Ur of the Chaldees (Acts 7:2. Compare Genesis 11:31 with 15:7; Joshua 24:2; Nehemiah 9:7). As we read carefully what is said, we find that this covenant was probably reiterated in Haran. Some writers have criticized Abraham for delaying his journey to Canaan. They believe that he was insensitive to God's command. Such views are both harsh and inaccurate. On the one hand, Abraham may have been delayed in Haran on account of his father's illness; and on the other, it shows us God's patience. If God dealt with us as severely as Abraham's critics deal with him, we would be in a sorry state, for we would be too fearful of offending Him to do anything.

At an appropriate time God reiterated His call. The covenant He entered into with Abraham was both gracious and unconditional. Abraham did nothing to deserve it. All he had to do was obey God. And God promised him blessings greater than anything he could have imagined: A land of his own, numerous children (an astounding promise inasmuch as Sarah was barren!), and assurance that all the families of the earth would be blessed through him. To better understand all of this, take a careful look at the following outline:

### ANALYSIS OF GENESIS 12:1-3

*Now the Lord said to Abram—*

*Go forth from your country*
> *your relatives*
> *your father's house*
> *to the land which I will show you.*

*And I will make you a great nation*
*And I will bless you and*
> *make your name great, and*
> *you shall be a blessing.*
> *And I will bless those who bless you*
> *And the one who curses you I will curse.*

*And in you all the families of the earth shall be blessed.*

OUTLINE

Introduction: God's Gracious Command

I. Separation Commanded
   A. From All That Has Characterized the Past
      1. Your Country
      2. Your Relatives
      3. Your Father's House.
   B. Details of the Promise
      1. National Blessings
      2. Personal Blessings

a. Blessings enjoyed

b. Blessings passed on

c. Assurance of protection.

3. Universal Blessings

But someone will ask, "Of what relevance is this to us today?" When God calls us to Himself, He enters into the same kind of gracious covenant. He promises that those who renounce their past ways and accept the salvation freely offered by Jesus Christ will be given eternal life (John 3:15-16, 36; 5:24; 10:28; 17:3; etc.) and that they will be made heirs of all the glories of His Kingdom (Romans 8:17; Galatians 3:29; Ephesians 3:6; Titus 3:7; James 2:5).

In the same way that God's covenant with Abraham was unilateral, so is His promise to us. We cannot do anything to merit the blessings He offers us.

But there's more. The covenant God made with Abraham is important for it enhances our understanding of other portions of Scripture. For example, the *"land"* that God promised to give to Abraham is enlarged in the Palestinian Covenant (Deuteronomy 28-30); the *"seed"* that God assured Abraham he would have is described in the Davidic Covenant (II Samuel 7:12-16); and the promise of blessing to *"all the families of the world"* is treated in the New Covenant (Jeremiah 31:31-34)—the covenant that the Lord Jesus instituted on the night of His betrayal.

These brief verses at the beginning of Genesis 12 are vital to our being able to grasp the plan and purpose of God[2] (cf. Romans 11:33).

*Travel With a **Purpose***

Now, as we look at Genesis 12:4-13:4, we are tempted to conclude that finding anything that resembles a "love letter" in these verses is impossible. Yet we also admit that they are part of inspired Scripture and need to be considered quietly, meditatively, and patiently, so that we can be open to the things the Lord will reveal to us. As we do so, we will see in God's dealings with Abraham, set against his travels to Canaan, a mirror of His love-relationship with us.

In an earlier chapter, we alluded to Abraham and Sarah's travels from Ur at the southern end of the Tigris-Euphrates River valley to Haran. When they left Ur with their aged father and Lot, Abraham's brother's son, Abraham was 75 years old, and Sarah was 60. They probably followed the course of the Euphrates River as they began their journey. If so, then they would have passed by Babylon and Mari before arriving at Haran. You can read about these cities and the people who lived in them in your Bible dictionary.[3] It will help you understand their customs and culture.

---

[2] For a discussion of these matters, see J. D. Pentecost's *Thy Kingdom Come* (1990), 360pp.

[3] The late M. F. Unger was an archaeologist and Bible scholar. The *New Unger's Bible Dictionary*, edited by R. K. Harrison, provides

After leaving Haran, the Lord led Abraham and Sarah south. They passed through Aleppo, may have visited Damascus (where Abraham possibly bought a slave named Eliezer, see Genesis 15:2), and then journeyed on. Did they cross the River Jordan above the Sea of Galilee or continue south to the River Jabbok where years later Jacob would ford the Jordan? We do not know, but inasmuch as Abraham was unfamiliar with the country it seems likely that he crossed at the first fordable place.

Abraham and Sarah traveled with a large retinue that could have approximated 2,000 men, women and children.[4] Camping would have posed a problem. Did Abraham send scouts on ahead to seek out the most suitable route and also locate a level place for their tents with good pasturelands for their sheep, cattle, goats and camels? The answer is most likely, yes. Such a large number would require considerable space, and setting up and breaking camp would take time. It is possible that they remained in one spot until Abraham's scouts returned and told him of the next convenient place.

In all probability as Abraham and Sarah moved south from Haran, they followed the Orontes River that runs between the Lebanon and Anti-Lebanon mountains. What

---

excellent articles on each of these cities as well as describing the customs and culture of the people.

[4] Genesis 14:14 mentions Abraham's trained fighting force of 318 men. If each man was married and had only one wife and no more than three children, this would equal 1,590. To this figure must be added Abraham's other servants who stayed behind and were not a part of this elite group—those who gathered wood, drew water, looked after all of the livestock, etc. A figure of 2,000 souls seems quite reasonable.

impressions filled their minds as they gazed up at snow-capped Mt. Hermon? Then, when they came abreast of the Sea of Galilee, do you think they considered settling on the fertile slopes of the hills that run down to this inland lake? Abraham might have been tempted to do so, but something impelled him to move on. We next read that they came to Shechem and attempted to settle there. Shechem is situated at the "navel" of the land at the pass between Mt. Ebal and Mt. Gerizim—a place known today as Tell Balata (cf. Genesis 33:18-20). There Abraham built an altar and called on the name of the Lord.

Many writers have commented on the fact that Abraham's life seems to be characterized by a *tent* and an *altar*. He was obviously engaged in a spiritual quest, otherwise he and Sarah could easily have stayed at Ur. Abraham's servants could then have looked after his flocks and herds. The "tent" indicates that he was a pilgrim and the "altar" (a more permanent structure) points to his worship of the One who had appeared to him. And Sarah shared his spiritual quest. Hebrews 11:8-10 informs us that it was *"by faith Abraham ... obeyed by going out to a place which he was to receive for an inheritance; and he went out, not knowing where he was going. By faith he lived as an alien in the land of promise, as in a foreign land, dwelling in tents with Isaac and Jacob, fellow heirs of the same promise; for he was looking for the city which has foundations, whose architect and builder is God."* He and his descendants did not receive the promises God made to them in their lifetimes, *but "welcomed them from a distance, having confessed that they were strangers and exiles on the earth.... And indeed if they had been thinking of that country from which they went out, they would have had opportunity to return. But as it is, they desire a better country, that is, a heavenly one. Therefore God is not ashamed to be called their God; for He has prepared a city for them"* (Hebrews 11:13-16).

Abraham felt uncomfortable so close to Shechem, and Moses adds a word of explanation: *"The Canaanite lived in the land."* There was something about the character and conduct of the Canaanites that Abraham found displeasing, and so he moved on. His example has been followed by Christian parents through the years. When moving to a new part of the country, they carefully check out places where they may wish to live. If their investigation reveals that the behavior and attitudes of the people would be detrimental to their children, they have done what Abraham did and moved on. Jacob failed to learn from his grandfather's example, and when he camped near Shechem, his daughter, Dinah, was raped (Genesis 34:1-5).

The next place Abraham and Sarah came to was Bethel, 20 miles south of Shechem. It was close to Ai. There he built an altar and worshipped the Lord. The Lord may not have given him any clear guidance, and so he continued his southward journey. He was still seeking. Upon reaching the Negev (literally, "the south country")—an area 22 miles south of Jerusalem and southwest of the Dead Sea, with Hebron as its principal commercial center—he finally felt sufficiently at ease to stay. While this area is dry and barren today, archaeologists have shown that in Abraham's day there were numerous springs in the area and the land was dotted with small villages. It would have been ideal for the needs of Abraham and his livestock. And thankful that he and Sarah had finally found a place in which to live, they settled down.

### *A Test of Faith*

It may have seemed to Abraham and Sarah as if they had only just "unpacked" when a famine decimated the land. Famines were not uncommon in Canaan in the period of the patriarchs (note Genesis 26:1; 41:56). If the November/December rains failed, then the springs dried up and the grass that the animals depended on for food withered and died. A herder such as Abraham could easily lose all his cattle in a single season. His sheep and goats, however, might survive.

Instead of waiting for calamity to overtake him, Abraham decided to journey to Egypt. He had probably heard that there was ample grazing land along the Nile. Many writers have severely criticized Abraham for forsaking the land to which the Lord had led him. They have built in to the words "went down" all sorts of lessons on backsliding. But typology has nothing to do with Abraham's actions. In going to Egypt, Abraham had to descend from the uplands of the Negev to the Valley of the Nile.

There was a problem that faced Abraham, however, and that was his beautiful wife, Sarah. He had probably heard of powerful Egyptians killing a woman's husband in order to take his wife.[5] En route to Egypt, Abraham persuaded Sarah to collaborate with him in an act of deception. She was to say that she was his "sister." This

---

[5] There is a papyrus in the British Museum that records how a Pharaoh living slightly later than the time of Abraham sent an army to the city of a man who had a beautiful wife with instructions to kill the husband and bring the woman to him!

was not a lie in the strict sense of the word, for she was his half-sister, but their intent was to deceive. Abraham knew that anyone wanting to marry Sarah would be obliged to negotiate the marriage with her father; and if he were dead, then with her brother. And Abraham could draw out the negotiations and, when all else failed, ask for a prohibitive dowry.

On one of our trips to Israel, there were two families in our group, each of which had a teenage daughter. One day in Old Jerusalem, an Arab youth approached the father of one young girl and offered him 50 camels for his daughter. The father was taken aback by the offer, and of course declined. When we were all back in the bus en route to our hotel, we were told of what had happened and thought that the whole incident was very amusing. The other father had all night to think of what he might say if similarly approached. It so happened that the next day we were in Bethlehem when a young Arab pushed his way through the crowd and asked this father, "What do you want for your daughter?" His reply was brief and to the point. "Don't talk to me about camels. I'm from America and I don't have any use for camels. How many oil wells will you give me?" At first the Arab was startled by the response. Then muttering curses in Arabic he quickly disappeared into the crowd.

It is possible that Abraham had a similar plan in mind. As Sarah's brother, he could ask a prohibitive dowry or discourage a possible suitor with innumerable delays. He did not realize that the Egyptians followed a custom that differed from what he was used to.

In Egypt, God unmasked Abraham's deceitful plan. He was exposed and forced to leave in disgrace. He remembered his stop to worship the Lord at Bethel, and returned there. The famine was still just as severe as it was before, and he had to rely on the Lord for his daily needs.

## *Hidden Treasures*

We now have to ask ourselves, "In what possible ways can this information resemble a love letter?" If we change Kierkegaard's initial idea of a love letter between sweethearts to a loving letter from a father to His child, then we come closer to understanding the mind of God. As a loving Father, he has our welfare at heart, and it is His desire to guide us in the path of His choosing.

First, Abraham's journey from Ur to the Negev took many months, and as we learn more of the country through which he passed, we can focus attention on the physical features of the land (i.e., different places, rainfall, productivity of the land, and special phenomena like mountains, lakes, rivers, plateaus, etc.), and the location of different cities with information about their size and the composition of their inhabitants. An enormous amount of information can be obtained from a good Bible dictionary. These cities and places may have had a great deal to offer Abraham and Sarah culturally, but spiritually they were not what God had in mind for them. As attractive as they may have been, therefore, the Lord did not permit them to stop in or near any of them.

Second, we need to ask ourselves what message Abraham's travels and experiences may have for us. Let us remember that Abraham and Sarah were on a pilgrimage. Abraham as head of the household (under his father) was responsible for making decisions. We may be sure that he shared with Sarah all that had taken place. His response to the revelation God gave him is important. It was immediate. *"He went forth as the Lord had spoken to him."* This was an act of faith.

We also need to notice the faithfulness of God. *"Abraham and Sarah set out to go to the land of Canaan; and into the land of Canaan they came"* (Genesis 13:5). Though the journey took many months, God remained faithful. And in a multitude of ways He showed them the way.

Often when God has been dealing with us we, too, step out in faith, trusting Him in much the same way Abraham did. But we are unsure of His leading. We expect Him to always lead us in the same way. How did God lead Abraham? Sometimes He appeared to him and spoke to him directly. At other times, Abraham built an altar and the Lord did not speak to him. This forced him to fall back on God's original command and obey it. And then there were times when Abraham had to rely on his own instincts and powers of observation.

Today God leads us through His Word (Psalm 119:105). There was no portion of the Bible extant in Abraham's day, so he did not have the Word of God to guide him. The method God chose was personal. And if Abraham stepped out of line, the Lord graciously brought him back into fellowship with Himself (cf. Proverbs 12:28; contrast 13:15; 16:25). From this, we realize that God is flexible.

The Lord also protected Abraham and his retinue on their journey. It would have been easy for robbers in the hills to sweep down on Abraham's encampment at night or attack his shepherds with speed and drive off his sheep. In keeping with His promise, the Lord protected Abraham and all that he had so that no one harmed him. And He brought them all safely into the land. What a stimulus this is to our faith! As a loving Father His care for us is constant.

Now consider His attitude. He treated Abraham as an intelligent human being, and He treats us the same way. He does not regulate our lives so that He overrides our wills, nor does He expect some "knee jerk" response from us. He delights in our remaining in fellowship with Him. Take a look at 13:6-10. *"Abraham passed through the land."* At each convenient stopping place, he must have weighed the pros and cons of settling there. Having no inner peace or instructions to the contrary, he moved on. God neither gave him marching orders each day nor forced him to stay in a particular place. He allowed Abraham freedom of choice (cf. Genesis 24:1*b*; 25:8).

In dealing with us, the Lord desires to bring us to full maturity. As we learn more of His ways, our choices will be more in keeping with what we have come to know of His will.

Note, too, how Abraham's spiritual sensitivity was sharpened as he considered the prospect of settling near Shechem. He was troubled. God knew this (as He knows of your concerns and mine) and met with His servant. He took the initiative and came to meet with him and strengthen him. And He does the same with us, only the means He often uses is His Word (cf. Psalm 119:105).

Upon reaching Bethel, Abraham sensed the need for fresh guidance. He built an altar. This time God did not meet with him. Apparently God intended Abraham to learn from the principles taught him during their last encounter. If this is so, then in all probability Abraham had to journey on with unresolved tensions. His experience at this point parallels our own, for we often pray for guidance only to find ourselves compelled to walk by faith.

Is God capricious? No. He is a loving Father. Often, however, He wisely withholds direct intimation of His will in order to deepen our trust in Him. We cannot grow spiritually if the path we tread is devoid of difficulties. Only when our course is strewn with obstacles are we kept in a position of humble dependence upon Him. Such was Abraham's experience as he journeyed on, not knowing where he would eventually settle.

We have all been on vacations and had our children ask, "Are we there yet?" Can you imagine Sarah asking Abraham, "How much longer? How will you know when we've arrived at the right place? Can't we just settle here? I'm tired of packing and unpacking, packing and unpacking our things."

Abraham finally reached the Negev. There he found everything conducive to his needs. He remained near the *"oak trees of Mamre"* in the general vicinity of Hebron. In this, too, we find a lesson for our earthly lives. When we find peace and relative freedom from anxiety, we should not expect that from this time onward our lives will be immune from testing. We'd like such a blissful existence to last indefinitely. But times of peace and tranquility seldom last for long. Abraham experienced a severe trial that threatened to rob him and Sarah of their livelihood. His faith was tested. Testing, however, isn't bad (cf. James 1:2-4). It is God's method of refining us and furthering our spiritual growth. We get so preoccupied with maintaining the status quo that we try by all means possible to eliminate adversity from our lives (note Peter's admonition in I Peter 1:5-9).

With God's help, Abraham and all that he had survived the famine.

## INTERACTION

1. As you reread Genesis 12:1-13:4, pay special attention to the connectives (e.g., "now," "so," "and," "then," etc.). Determine whether these connectives indicate time, place, emphasis, explanation, contrast, continuation, reason, result, purpose, contrast, or condition.

2. Pretend that you are either Abraham or Sarah. Write a letter to your relatives in Haran describing your journey since leaving them. You will find information from Question 1 helpful. A Bible dictionary will give you data about the physical features and places. If you are meeting with a group, share your insights with them.

3. As you continue your study of Genesis 12:10-13:4, seek to determine in what way God may be using the experience of either Abraham (see Hebrews 11:8-10) or Sarah (see I Peter 3:1-6) to further your spiritual growth.

Chapter Six

# WINDOW ON THE WORLD

## THE HISTORICAL METHOD

History can be fascinating, and no historical record is more fascinating or diverse than the one contained in the Bible. As we come to grips with the history of the people of God, we have the opportunity to pass beyond the surface details and sense inwardly the hopes and fears, feelings and aspirations, longings and shortcomings of people as real as you and I (cf. James 5:17*a*). Like us, they ate and drank, loved and hated, faced adversity and at times enjoyed prosperity; cherished personal desires, struggled with priorities and endured the endless round of daily tasks.

***Where to Begin***
The historic method of Bible study can be applied to a book (e.g., Genesis, or books like Joshua through II Chronicles, the Gospels, and Acts) or to a person (e.g., Abraham and Sarah, Moses, Ruth, Esther, Paul, Christ) or an incident (e.g., the Flood, the giving of the Ten Commandments, the Sermon on the Mount, or Paul's address to the philosophers in Athens), et cetera. As we begin, we must of necessity take a careful look at the setting and find out all we can about the people, events and places referred to in the biblical record. In addition, we must apply the principles of Bible study learned in earlier chapters of this work (viz., *observation, interpretation,*

*application*) so that we can accurately weigh the information before us and uncover the attitude of nations or the intent of different people. We must also discover as much as we can about what life was like in those days, where people lived, the kind of houses they lived in, what they did for a living, to whom they were responsible, and the social, political, economic, and religious trends that prevailed.[1]

In addition, we need to develop a chronological framework so that we can relate what was taking place in one part of the world to the rise and development of kingdoms elsewhere. In this connection, I remember reading about an experience of the late Dr. Harry Rimmer, for many years president of the Research Science Bureau. The incident he relates took place when he was a student in a college in California.

> The teacher of the course, Professor Rosenberger, was one of the ablest pedagogues who ever wasted her life in the more or less important task of teaching a rising generation how to think! At the end of the first few weeks in a class in English history, she informed the student group that the following day we would be privileged to have a test in this particular subject. When the class gathered for the happy event, there were twenty questions that were to constitute our examination.
>
> The first question was something like this, "What new treaty had just been signed between

---

[1] In this connection a great deal of information can be gleaned from Vos' *New Illustrated Bible Manners and Customs* (1999), 661pp.

France and Spain that had a bearing on this particular period?"

The next question had to do with the political commitments of the Holy Roman Empire.

The third question took us into the Germanic states, and in all of the twenty questions not one word concerning England!

As the class sat with the usual and habitual expression of vacuity that generally adorns the countenance of a college student facing a quiz, the Professor said, "You may begin."

Some hapless wit procured the courage to protest, by saying, "But you said this was to be an examination in English history." To which Professor Rosenberger replied, "Quite so! This is English history!" Then leaning forward over the desk she said, in impressive tones, "How can you expect to know what England is doing, and why, if you do not know the pressure upon her of her enemies and friends at that particular period?"

A long distance back in our mental vacuum a dim light began to glow, and we were never caught that way again! When the teacher said French history, we read everything else! When she said German history, we specialized on the surrounding countries. One day as we were thinking over this delightful technique of understanding, the idea began to grow that if this is the proper way to study secular history, *it ought to apply to the Bible as well!*

There is an illumination that brightens the meaning of the Sacred Text when read in the light of collateral events that can come in no other way.[2]

## *The Grand Design*

When applied to an entire book of the Bible, the historic method seeks to answer the questions, When was the book written? Why was it written? By whom was it written, and for whom was it intended? Then we also need to ask and answer the question, Where was the book written and how did its message meet the needs of those who first received it? Finally, there is the often disturbing question, What relevance does this book have for us today?

We will find that the historic method of Bible study has many benefits. For example, it will ground our faith in the objective facts of history. It will enlarge our concept of the reality and presence of God and His intimate knowledge of the things that are of concern to us. It will also challenge our faith as we contemplate the future, and at the same time give us confidence based on God's involvement with His people in the past. And it will illustrate for us the lessons of history, and total up the price that is extracted when history's warnings are ignored.

The historical method of Bible study may also be applied to an historic incident (in the experience of a person or tribe or nation). For example, when we survey the circumstances leading up to a specific event (e.g., the birth of Christ, cf. Galatians 4:4) or consider the results of an

---

[2] H. Rimmer, *Dead Men Tell Tales* (1945), 15-17.

significant incident (like the fall of Jerusalem, see Luke 21:24), we need to understand as fully as possible what happened, what led up to or caused this event, the contribution of what happened to subsequent events, and how what we have read ties in with the theme of the book.

## *Return to the Land*

After Abraham's sojourn in the land of Egypt, he returned to Canaan. Lot, of course, had accompanied him to the land of the Nile and journeyed back to Bethel with him. Once they had settled in the land, trouble broke out (see Genesis 13:1-18). Lot was rich in his own right. Their herdsmen began quarreling over the available pasture land. So much bitterness ensued that Abraham called Lot aside and suggested magnanimously that they separate. He offered Lot first choice. Lot, as we know, chose the well-watered plain of the River Jordan. There were cities in the valley where he could sell farm produce and buy some of the things he may have missed since leaving Ur. It was a selfish choice. He should have insisted that his uncle choose first. But Lot, wanting the best for himself, chose what appeared to be the best place. Abraham remained in the highlands, relatively free from outside influence.

Lot had chosen hastily. He hadn't spent too many months in his new surroundings when he began to realize that the people of Sodom had to pay very high taxes. A foreign king named Chedorlaomer, King of Elam, had placed them under heavy tribute. In spite of this, he prospered. At first he *only "pitched his tent toward Sodom,"* but it wasn't long before he took up residence in the city.

Lot stands out on the pages of God's Word as a person who wanted to be rich. He apparently felt that riches would bring him a sense of security. Abraham, by contrast, was content with what God gave him and was secure in his relationship with the Lord. That is why he was prepared to give Lot first choice of the land. But Lot's choice was a bad one. Moses inserts an "editorial comment" in verse 13: *"Now the men of Sodom were wicked exceedingly and sinners against the Lord."*

## *Renewal of the Covenant*

But what of the covenant God had made with Abraham? Hadn't He promised to give Abraham the land? The Lord hadn't forgotten His covenant, and His promise to give Canaan to Abraham was unconditional. That is why He came to His faithful servant and said, *"Now lift up your eyes and look from the place where you are, northward and southward and eastward and westward; for all the land which you see, I will give it to you and to your descendants forever. I will make your descendants as the dust of the earth, so that if anyone can number the dust of the earth, then your descendants can also be numbered. Arise, walk about the land through its length and breadth; for I will give it to you."*

## *More Than a Border Fracas*

We now come to Genesis 14. Few portions of Scripture enable us to see the benefits of historical study more clearly than this one. Up until now we have been concerned with Abraham and Sarah and their journeys. All of a sudden, we are compelled to become acquainted with four kings from the East. Who were they? Where did they live? Why did they attack Sodom and Gomorrah?

Some of the answers to these questions can be obtained from a good Bible atlas. At least one answer comes from the text itself. We are told that the cities of the plain *"served"* Chedorlaomer (i.e., paid tribute to him). They were his vassals; he was their suzerain. For twelve years, they begrudgingly paid these "taxes," but in the thirteenth year they rebelled. They did not send him the usual "present."[3] Knowing the might of Chedorlaomer, the kings of the city-states of Sodom and Gomorrah formed an alliance with three other small kingdoms. They now felt that they could hold their own against Chedorlaomer's army.

Did Chedorlaomer learn of this alliance, and is this why he obtained the help of three allies? Though this question cannot be answered with finality now, it is worthy of consideration. Perhaps the spade of some future archaeologist will unearth the answer.

## *Testimony of the Spade*

Genesis 14:5 records the route taken by the four kings of the east. It is of historic interest. For many years, critics of the Bible scorned all thought of an invading army following the line of march mentioned in Scripture, and those who accepted the biblical record were vilified. These detractors also claimed that no such extensive travel existed as would be necessary for such a military expedition.

---

[3] A euphemism used in ancient texts to describe the tribute sent to a king.

We'll take up the second criticism first. Evidence concerning extensive travel in the days of Abraham comes from a clay tablet found at Mari. It specifically stipulates that a wagon rented in Mari must not be driven to the coast of the Mediterranean Sea. This incidental piece of evidence confirms that travel from Mesopotamia to the Mediterranean was a common occurrence.

But what of the route taken by the kings of the East? A Jewish archaeologist named Dr. Nelson Glueck has provided us with the answer. He writes:

> Archaeology has buttressed the accuracy of the Biblical account of the existence and destruction of this long line...of cities by the kings of the East. Particularly remarkable and worthy of special emphasis is the fact that all of them were destroyed at the end of the nineteenth century B.C., with only a few of them ever being reoccupied.[4]

The question arises, Why did Amraphael, Arioch, Chedorlaomer and Tidal destroy the cities east of the River Jordan (Genesis 14:5-6)? Did they fear an alliance between them and other kings that might cut off their homeward march? Captives taken when outward bound would have hindered the conquerors' invasion of the area around the southern end of the Dead Sea when speed was of the essence.[5] Their primary objective was Sodom and Gomorrah; they wished to instill fear in the hearts of the people living in the plain by destroying their eastern neighbors.

---

[4] Glueck, *Rivers in the Desert*, 6-9, 74.

[5] See Yigael Yadin, *The Art of Warfare in Bible Lands* (1963), I:40-45.

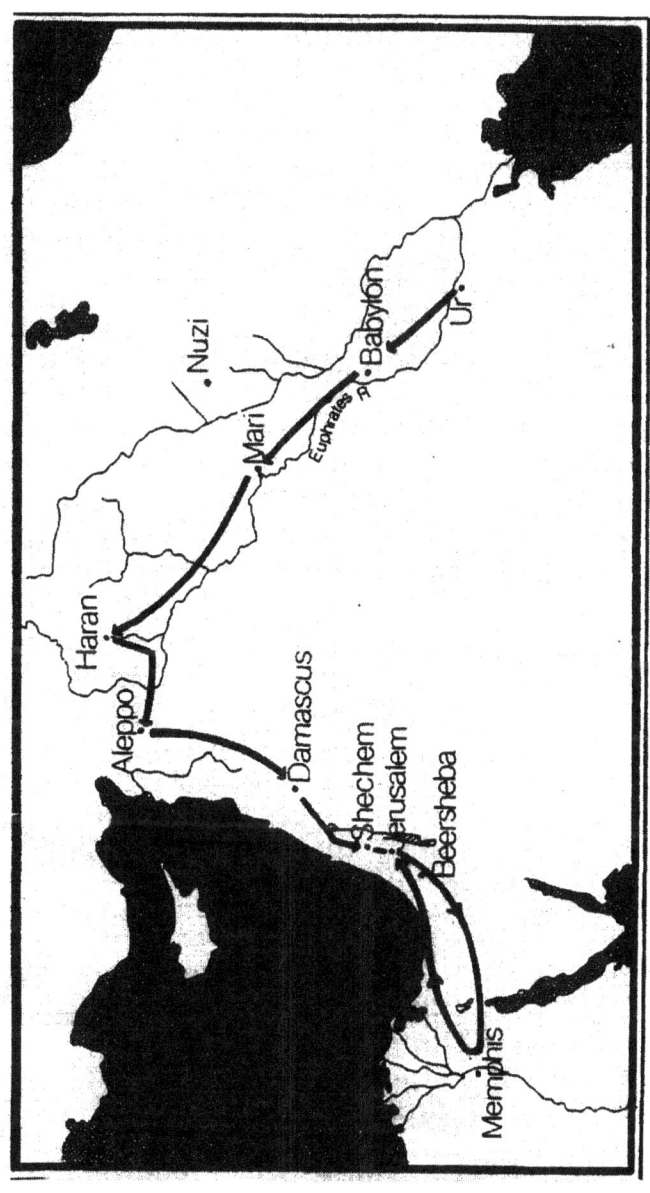

## *The Warning Ignored*

Now the scene changes. Our attention shifts to the kings of Sodom and Gomorrah (Genesis 14:8). They appear confident and take the initiative by going out to meet the invaders. They also chose the site for the coming battle—the Valley of Siddim. Did they think that once routed, the tar pits would serve their ends and make the defeat of the invaders complete? Probably so.

When the battle began, the five kings of the valley found themselves unable to hold their own. As the people of Asia and Eastern Europe would later give way before the might of Attila the Hun, so these kings gave way before the superior power of Chedorlaomer. They fled in disarray. Instead of the tar pits working to their advantage, these slimy traps were the means of their undoing. Such is the short-lived confidence of the proud of heart.

## *Hope for Peace and Prosperity*

Lot is now reintroduced into the story (Genesis 14:12). By the time of the attack, he had taken up residence in Sodom. We are left to assume that trade had probably expanded to such an extent that he was needed in the "home office" so that he could better superintend his expanding monopoly.

But how do you think he felt when the city was attacked and the walls breached? And what do you think passed through his mind when, bound and a captive, and with all of the wealth he had labored to acquire in the hands of foreigners, he was led away to be sold as a slave?

Lot may not have been conscious of God's involvement in his life as he was pushed and prodded along the dusty road by his captors. But God had not forgotten him. As a believer (see II Peter 2:7), he was to benefit from the blessings of the Abrahamic Covenant. In order that these blessings might be fulfilled, the Lord allowed a lone servant of Lot's to escape. How and where he hid from those who were ransacking Sodom has not been told us. We do know that, as soon as it was safe, he hastened to Abraham.

The Dead Sea is situated about 1,290 feet below sea level. Hebron, near the oaks of Mamre, is over 3,000 feet above sea level. Only 25 miles separate the two places. The terrain, however, is hilly, with steep cliffs and deep ravines. The fact that the servant reached Abraham, and that Abraham overtook the kings by the time they reached Dan, shows how rapidly the servant brought the news to Abraham, and how speedily Abraham and his allies traveled to Dan.

## *Fulfillment of the Covenant*

When the Lord entered into a covenant with Abraham, He assured him that *"those who blessed him would be blessed, and those who cursed him would be cursed."* Now God shows that He is as good as His word.

Abraham, we find, is well-known and well-liked, and living peaceably among the Amorites (Genesis 14:13). He has also formed an alliance with them.[6] Upon hearing the

---

[6] Probably a blood covenant in which each, though retaining their independence, promised to help and support the other for as long as they lived. See Trumbull, *The Blood Covenant* (1978), 267-69, 322.

news, Abraham, his trained militia, and his allies set out in pursuit of Chedorlaomer. It is a long, forced march. Finally, they overtake Chedorlaomer and his army near Dan. There Abraham organizes a pincer movement, and having the advantage of surprise, he utterly routs the invaders.

Why were the forces of Chedorlaomer so vulnerable? Could it be that they were careless because they thought they had killed everyone who might hinder their homeward journey?

*A Hero's* **Welcome**

On his way back to Sarah and his encampment at Mamre, Abraham and his men pass by Salem (the ancient name for Jerusalem). They are weary and in need of rest. Melchizedek (a name derived from two Hebrew words: *melek*, "king" and *zedek*, "righteousness), king of Salem (from *shalom*, "peace") and priest of *El Elyon*, "God Most High," comes to meet Abraham. He offers him and those with him refreshment and blesses Abraham in the name of *"God Most High."*

Apart from this historic reference to Melchizedek, we know nothing of this king-priest from Jerusalem. What transpires between Melchizedek and Abraham, however, is of great significance, and Hebrews 7 (note vv. 1, 3, 15-25) builds the priesthood of Christ upon this incident. As such, these verses are of importance to us as we build a biblical doctrine of the Person of Christ. As we read on, we note to our surprise that Abraham gives Melchizedek tithes of the spoils (cf. Hebrews 7:2-4, 10).[7] The writer of Hebrews uses this incident to show that Melchizedek's priesthood was greater than the Aaronic priesthood, and that Christ's priesthood is patterned after Melchizedek's.

As Abraham began the twenty-two-mile journey south, he probably reflected on the events that had transpired. He had also come to appreciate God in a whole new way—as *El Elyon, "God Most High."*

It is as a result of the historic method of Bible study that we, too, come to experience God in a whole new way. Our appreciation of His involvement in our lives is enhanced as we see Him working behind the scenes. This is illustrated for us in His care of Lot. From a callous, human point of view, it might be said, "Well, Lot got what he deserved. No one twisted his arm and forced him to live in Sodom. Had he maintained his integrity and not been lured into the city in the pursuit of wealth, he would not have been placed in a compromising position, and he would have been spared the evils that befell the city."

But such a view ignores human nature. It overlooks the fact that there is something of Lot in each one of us. We want to serve the Lord, but we also want to enjoy the benefits of wealth and enjoy the power that accompanies riches. A conflict takes place within us and, as with Lot, we attempt to rationalize the situation. Then, sooner or later, we resort to compromise. God, however, is at work behind the scenes. Though He may chasten us, He also

---

[7] The kings of the East had acquired considerable spoil from the cities they destroyed on the eastern side of the River Jordan, and from their conquest of Mount Seir. The riches taken from Sodom and Gomorrah were returned to the people living in the plain of Jordan.

gives us another opportunity to live a godly life and honor Him.

The historical method of Bible study also reveals to us the multi-faceted personality of Abraham. He was content with the things the Lord had given him. He was also a compassionate man, a strong leader, a person of influence in the community, and a man possessing rare spiritual sensitivity. Note how he handled the king of Sodom (Genesis 14:21-24). It was very flattering to be greeted by the king of Sodom in *"the King's Valley."* The record is very brief. It shows Abraham's strong resolve. He refused to enrich himself from the legitimate spoils of war, and this prevented him from becoming ensnared in political entanglements. Had he not done so, Sodom's ruler would have tacitly taken credit for Abraham's newly found wealth.

Abraham had to make this refusal in a firm, definite way. To betray even the slightest vacillation would have shown the king of Sodom a weakness that he could then exploit to his advantage. His offer could then have been renewed with the reward raised.

Abraham was a wise leader. We observe that he was also mindful of others. When he had entered into a covenant with Mamre, he did not impose his values on those among whom he lived. And after defeating the eastern alliance, he insured that the Amorites and their men were allowed to take what was rightfully theirs.

## *Human Need*

But where does this brief rehearsal of the facts leave you and me?

Initially, we are left overawed by the fact that our God cares for us and has the ability to meet our needs, no matter what they may be. And this, of course, is beautifully illustrated for us in this chapter. Lot did not deserve God's favor, yet it was extended to him. Even when he was filled with fear, deprived of his autonomy, chained to other prisoners and stumbling toward a life of slavery, God was at work to accomplish his deliverance. And in the Hebrew youth who ran to the camp of Abraham, we see God's use of means to accomplish His ends.

This story also illustrates the trials by which God, as a loving Father, seeks to wean us away from the allurement of this world and its passing pleasures (see Hebrews 11:25-26; 12:5-13) to a life of faith!

How aptly the maturity of a believer is illustrated for us in the case of Abraham, who, while living a life of separation to God, nevertheless was able to enjoy warm relationships with those around him! His alliance with the Amorites was not one of compromise, but of mutual benefit. They respected him for who he was, a man of integrity, and they gladly followed him when he set out to rescue Lot. How well this pictures the influence a Christian may have on those about him.

## INTERACTION

1. By using a Bible dictionary, a Bible concordance, and your Bible, research the historic background of each incident in this chapter. Be sure to discuss your findings with someone in your study group or with a friend.

2. Make a chart by paragraphs of Genesis 15-17. Take note of the specific sections within this division, observing the relationships between paragraphs, etc. Give headings to each paragraph and section. Finally, provide a heading for this segment of Abraham's life.

Chapter Seven

# SPANNING THE CENTURIES

## THE CULTURAL APPROACH

In the Preface, I quoted from Charles C. Ryrie's Introduction to the Ryrie Study Bible in which he reminds us that "The Bible is the greatest of all books; to study it is the noblest of all pursuits; to understand it, the highest of all goals." Dr. Ryrie's admonition is timely, and his words deserve to be taken seriously.

The Bible is a part of our Christian heritage, and the stories many of us heard as we grew up are permeated with important truths. But even the accounts of Joseph and his "coat of many colors," Moses being taken out of the River Nile by Pharaoh's daughter, Ruth gathering up leftover grain in the field of Boaz, David killing Goliath, Daniel being thrown into the lion's den, Esther saving her people, the Lord Jesus restoring the sight of the blind man, Paul writing his letters, or John being exiled to the island of Patmos, must be understood within their cultural context. We need to know how these people dressed, what kinds of food they ate, how they cultivated the land, the way in which their cities were governed, the function(s) of their religious leaders, the different observances they followed, what happened when another nation made war with them, the kinds of houses they lived in, what their furniture was made of, the marriage and family practices they followed, and the diverse occupations that were open to them.

Most of us spend more time in the New Testament than the Old, but how are we to interpret statements like the one in Luke's gospel of a person who called late one night asking for bread so as to be able to feed a visitor recently come to his home, only to be told by his friend, *"My children are with me in bed"*? (Luke 11:5); or John the Baptist eating locusts and wild honey? (Matthew 3:4); or the compliment paid the bridegroom at the wedding in Cana because he *"kept the good wine until the end"*? (John 2:10); or Christ's method of teaching with questions when He said, *"Are there not four months and then comes the harvest?"* (John 4:35); or Paul's shaving his head because he had taken a vow? (Acts 18:18), et cetera. An accurate interpretation of these and many other things we read about are all dependent upon a knowledge of the customs and culture of the people.

All of this points up the fact that one of the most fascinating and rewarding facets of Bible study is an awareness of the way people lived, worked, loved, saw children born into their homes, participated in religious and social events, grew old and eventually died. A cultural approach also helps us come to grips with the moral, intellectual, and social values of the people. And so, whether our interest is in art or music, architecture or literature, religion or philosophy, agriculture or politics, law or history, we cannot help but be fascinated by the events and circumstances that made up their lives.

In few places in Scripture do we find as rich and varied a cultural background as in the life and times of Abraham and Sarah. By birth, they were residents of southern Mesopotamia with its rich heritage derived from the Sumerians, its language adopted from the Akkadians, and its social practices influenced by the Amorites. As a result of this heritage, Abraham and Sarah probably spoke more than one language, and felt comfortable with people of different nationalities. Only among the hostile Canaanites did they feel ill at ease. Other people whom they encountered during their earthly pilgrimage included the Hurrians (or Horites) of the Fertile Crescent, the Egyptians, the Philistines, and the Hittites who lived near Hebron.

By occupation, Abraham, when he lived in Ur, was in all probability a merchant (as well as an owner of livestock). Ur was a leading commercial center. Caravans bringing goods from the West stopped there, and ships bringing a variety of merchandise from the Orient sailed into the Persian Gulf and docked at the harbor nearby. As a result, Abraham was able to deal with people of various ethnic backgrounds and businessmen in all walks of life. And Sarah enjoyed shopping for the latest silks and linens, perfumes and other cosmetics in the stores of Ur.

## *Changing Roles*

Once Abraham and Sarah moved to Canaan, all of this changed. He was no longer a "merchant prince" (as some have called him), but was now a "cattle rancher" who was dependent on the rainy season for the grass needed to keep his cattle and sheep, goats and camels alive. Consequently, when we read in the Bible of the *"former"* and *"latter"* rains we need to know when they occurred, why they were so necessary, and what happened if they were late or failed altogether. The *"former rains"* of late September/October were needed to make the land arable. Those who planted wheat and barley needed the rain to begin to germinate the seed they had sown. And the *"latter rains"* of March/April were essential if there was to be a bumper harvest (Deuteronomy 11:14).

Abraham and Sarah now lived in the Negev (or *"southland,"* bordering on the desert), having exchanged residence in a large house for rugs and cushions on the desert sand. And they needed the rains in order to keep the springs flowing freely so that they would have water for domestic use and so their livestock would have grass to eat and not die of thirst.

Abraham probably traded with an occasional caravan that passed by or sent his servants with donkeys or camels to a nearby town to buy whatever was needed. And we may be sure that Sarah looked forward to shopping in Hebron where she could purchase clothing and other "necessities." Included in her purchases were most certainly scented oils and perfumes for how else did she keep her skin soft and moist in the hot, dry desert air?

Cultural refinements, of course, were few. Sarah, however, was able to keep herself looking good (cf. I Peter 3:1-6; see Genesis 12:15; 20:1-10 for evidence of her attractiveness), and a knowledge of the culture of the times helps to explain how she did so.

## *Rule of Law*

**Politically.** The ancient Near East was ruled by petty kings who reigned over city-states. They usually established a dynasty and exercised power because they claimed to be ruling on behalf of the local deity. Some of these kings even claimed to be the son of the local god.

With each city being under the "lordship" of a king, and with cities varying in size and importance, it was common for smaller cities to band together so that, in the event of a war, their combined forces could more readily repel the invader (cf. Genesis 14:1-5). This is what happened when Chedorlaomer and his allies invaded the Jordan Valley.

Whenever a king went forth to war, he aroused the patriotic zeal of his followers by asserting that this war had been commanded by, or was in honor of, the local deity.[1] Archaeologists have unearthed royal libraries in which they found clay tablets summoning people to battle in the name of their god. In one case, where there may have been reluctance on the part of some to "volunteer," a man and his cattle were dismembered and their body parts carried throughout the empire. The message was clear: Join forces with the king or suffer a similar fate.

**Religiously.** The people of the ancient Near East were very superstitious. They had become addicted to idols. Each cultural center had its pantheon. There was, however, a principal deity. Ur was the residence of the moon-god, Sin; Babylon was the center of the cult of Ishtar; Nineveh boasted of a host of gods, the most feared of which was Nebo; the Canaanites worshipped El (though he was gradually eclipsed by Baal); the Hittites worshipped a winged bull with a man's head; and the Philistines adored the male and female deities, Baal and Astarte. These gods took on various characteristics, depending on the area; and everything that happened—whether good or bad—was

---

[1] Examples of this kind of conscription may be found in Pritchard's *Ancient Near Eastern Texts*, 294-301.

attributed to them.[2] These gods were capricious, licentious, and depraved; and the people became like them.[3]

**Sociologically.** The era in which Abraham lived was patriarchal. The patriarch was the head of the family. He possessed absolute power over the lives of his wives, children (including married children), and servants. Some modern writers would have us believe that this authority was exercised in a dictatorial manner. All the evidence that has come down to us indicates that family members were treated with respect, and that the leadership given the family by the patriarch was authoritative,[4] not coercive. Of course, there must have been exceptions then as there are now. We err, however, if we make the exceptions the rule and disregard all evidence to the contrary.

In the patriarchal age it was expected that the eldest son would take over the headship of the family upon his father's death. This is borne out in the life of Abraham. When God wished to bypass Ishmael in favor of the yet-unborn Isaac, Abraham protested, *"O that Ishmael might live in Your sight"* (Genesis 17:18). This request was denied.

---

[2] See the article of "Idolatry" in *Zondervan's Pictorial Encyclopedia of the Bible* (1975), III:242-48.

[3] Psalm 115:8 deals with those who make and worship idols (115:1-7). Verse 8 reads: "Those who make them will become like them, [so it will be with] everyone who trusts in them."

[4] In *Leadership: The Dynamics of Success* (1982), 126pp., the authors divide leadership into three primary categories: authoritarian, authoritative, and permissive.

In general, the rights of the firstborn, following the death of his father, included serving as the spiritual leader of the family. But there were exceptions. Ishmael was bypassed, and this privilege was bestowed on Isaac (Galatians 4:21-31). Later, when Isaac had children of his own, Esau, his firstborn, despised this privilege and sold his right to Jacob for a bowl of stew (Genesis 25:29-34).

Marriage within the extended family (cf. Abraham's marriage to his half-sister, Sarah [Genesis 20:12]; Isaac's marriage to his cousin [Genesis 24:1-9; contrast 26:34-35]); Jacob's taking a wife from his own relatives [Genesis 28:1-5]), broadened as time went by to include taking a wife from within one's tribe. In these early times, it was a father's duty to obtain a suitable wife for his son. Because Isaac was the son of Abraham's old age, and because he did not want Isaac to marry a Canaanite, Abraham commissioned his faithful servant to obtain a bride for Isaac.

A wife in patriarchal times (as now!) was the single most important member of the family. Both as wife and mother she was the homemaker and exerted considerable influence on her husband and children. The household servants were subject to her authority. Biblical references (e.g., Proverbs 31:10-31) indicate that she held an honored position, had a voice in family affairs, and could engage in commercial activities.[5]

---

[5] It is freely admitted that in time, and in certain cultures, her worth diminished. Even in Judaism men prayed daily "I thank Thee, O Lord, that you have not made me a slave, a Gentile, or a woman." But this is not the way it was. Eve, for example, shared equally with Adam the image and likeness of God (Genesis 1:26-27), and was the subject of the first love song in all of recorded history (Genesis 2:23). Sarah held an honored position in Abraham's household (Genesis 21:10, 12); Rebekah was loved by her husband (Genesis 27:46-28:1); the whole

When Abraham and Sarah left Haran for Canaan they *"lived in tents"* (literally, *"houses of hair"*). These tents were made of black or brown goat's hair. Their size and number depended on the growth of the family. The average tent was 10 feet by 15 feet, and was supported by nine poles. It was divided in half to separate the area of the husband and his sons from his wife and daughters. Guests were normally entertained outside the tent (Genesis 18:4, 10), but if they stayed overnight, they slept in the front part with the husband (Genesis 26:29-31).

As a man's family grew in size, and as additional wives were added, it often became necessary for each wife to have her own tent (see Genesis 30:15-16; 31:33). In time, a young man might have a tent of his own, to which, when he married, he brought his bride. Isaac, apparently, did not have a tent of his own. When he married Rebekah he moved into the tent that Sarah had formerly occupied (Genesis 24:67). (With Abraham's frequent absences from the encampment, she had probably set up a tent of her own.)

---

book of Ruth is a testimony to the dignity accorded women of character; Hannah stands out on the pages of Scripture as a great and gracious woman (I Samuel 1:1-2:10); and who can forget the wisdom of a woman such as Abigail (I Samuel 25:32-35). That the condition of women deteriorated over time is undisputed. In an agrarian economy sons were preferred to daughters. Christ and the teaching of the New Testament sought to correct this. For further information, see J. G. Mandley's *Woman Outside of Christendom* (1880), 159pp.

## Covenants and Promises

**The Promise of Protection.** As we look at Genesis 15-16, we find that the text is permeated with details that enlarge our knowledge of the culture of the times. The phrase *"after these things,"* connects the incidents that are described for us in the preceding chapter. There we read of Abraham's complete rout of the coalition of kings from the East. He then returned to the Negev in triumph. En route, the kings of the area acknowledged his victory. Why is it, then, that he was consumed with fear? In fact, so great was his apprehension that it became necessary for the Lord to come to him and say, *"Do not fear, Abraham; I am a shield to you."* What did Abraham fear?

It seems that he feared that the kings whom he had defeated would find out who it was who had so thoroughly trounced them, and next year, *"at the time when kings go forth to war,"* they would come looking for him.

But hadn't the kings of the city-states of Canaan greeted Abraham on his return? Didn't they give him a hero's welcome? Hadn't they honored him by meeting with him in the *"Valley of the King"*? Yes. All of this is true. Abraham, however, was not sociologically naïve. He knew the fickleness of those with whom he was dealing. Coercive pressures or a suitable bribe given an official or a peasant would be sufficient to loosen anyone's tongue and give Chedorlaomer all the information he required. Abraham had good reason to fear that this powerful monarch would come looking for him.

But wouldn't those who were glad to be rid of the invaders stand by the patriarch? Not likely. They would be more inclined to capitulate and agree to become Chedorlaomer's vassals once more. Abraham knew the culture too well to be deluded into relying on the Canaanites for support. He, therefore, had good cause to fear what might happen.

Was there anything in God's *"Fear not!"* to allay his emotions? Yes, there was. God is sovereign, and the only antidote to fear is to place ourselves unreservedly in His care, trusting in His sovereign goodwill toward us for our safety.

**The Promise of an Heir.** A second item of cultural importance comes to us as we consider Abraham's conversation with the Lord (Genesis 15:2-6). When God relieved Abraham's fears, this freed up his emotions and another burdensome matter surfaced. Ten years earlier God had promised Abraham a son. Childlessness carried with it a social stigma. Childless couples were thought to have offended the gods (or the God) in some way, and on account of their sin they were being punished by having children withheld from them. Abraham and Sarah believed God's promise. They left Ur and went to Canaan. Abraham maintained an unsullied testimony in the land. Why was Sarah still barren? And so he complains to the Lord, *"Of what value are all Your benefits to me, seeing I remain childless?"*

Before we condemn Abraham for his ingratitude, let us remember how often we have similarly complained about the Lord and His dealings with us. We become impatient under testing. Furthermore, Sarah was getting older. She wanted to please her husband by giving him what he desired most: a son. She would soon cease to ovulate. We know from what is revealed later on that this fear was very real.

Now note 15:2*b* and 3. It was quite apropos in their culture for a rich person and his wife to adopt a slave as their heir. Such a person would be regarded as their son and would have the status of one born in their house. Tablets unearthed by archaeologists at Nuzi have shed light on this custom. One adoption tablet reads:

> The tablet of adoption belonging to [Zike], the son of Akkuya: he gave his son Shennima in adoption to Shuriha-ilu, and Shuriha-ilu, with reference to Shennima, [from] all the lands ... [and] his earnings of every sort gave to Shennima one [portion] of his property. If Shuriha-ilu should have a son of his own, as the principal [son] he shall take a double share; Shennima shall then be next in order [and] take his proper share. As long as Shuriha-ilu is alive, Shennima shall revere him. When Shuriha-ilu [dies], Shennima shall become the heir.

It soon happened as Sarah expected. *"It ceased to be with her after the manner of women."* That is why, in chapter 16, she encouraged Abraham to take Hagar as a second wife. Her hope was that Hagar might conceive and bear a son. Then she and Abraham could adopt him as their own. Such a practice was fully in accord with the laws of their time. Another tablet contains the following:

> If a man's wife has not borne him children, [but] a harlot [from] the public square has borne him children, he shall provide grain, oil, and clothing for that harlot; the children which the harlot has borne him shall be his heirs, and as long

as his wife lives the harlot shall not live in the house with his wife.[6]

Hagar, of course, was not a prostitute. As we shall find later on, God did not intend that the Messianic line should run through her. Instead, wishing to assure Abraham of His faithfulness, the Lord met with him (Genesis 15:4*b*). The encounter probably took place in Abraham's tent at night, for God took him outside where they could look up into the clear, starlit sky. He then said to him: *"Count the stars. So shall your descendants be."* And Abraham believed God.

Of course, having this many descendants required that Abraham have a son to start the process. God then reminded Abraham that He had brought him out of the land of the Chaldeans to give him the land in which he was living. As yet, he did not possess so much as a fraction of an acre. This led Abraham to ask another question, *"O Lord God, how may I know that I shall possess it?"*

Verses 12-21 contain God's answer and the third cultural phenomenon mentioned in this chapter, namely, the blood covenant by which God pledged Himself to fulfill His word. This material builds upon God's earlier promise to Abraham (see 12:1-3), and enlarges upon God's promise of the land (*viz.*, Canaan).

**The Promise of the Land.** Culturally, covenants in the ancient Near East fell into two categories: Parity covenants (between equals) and suzerainty covenants (often

---

[6] See *Ancient Near Eastern Texts (1955)*, 172-74.

called treaties) between a superior (like a king) and the people of another region or nation who became his vassals.[7]

Normally there were two principal parties to these agreements. On rare occasions, however, a covenant could be instituted by one person, who would take upon himself all the conditions of the covenant. This is what happened in Genesis 15. God unilaterally took upon Himself the responsibility to fulfill all the conditions of the covenant.

It is important for us to notice the form of covenant that God chose. Of the different kinds of pacts,[8] God chose the most solemn. Verses 9-10 indicate what animals were to be brought and how they were to be divided and arranged. The fact that they had to be killed and then cut in half is important. The parties entering into such an agreement intimated that the same death and dismemberment would befall them if they failed to perform the obligations agreed upon.[9]

Normally, when everything was ready, the parties to the covenant would stand before the animals and go over the reasons for entering into this pact. Then, with the preliminaries to the covenant understood by both parties,

---

[7] See the article on "Covenants" in *Zondervan's Pictorial Encyclopedia of the Bible*, I:1001-03.

[8] The principal ones were the Salt Covenant, the Threshold Covenant, and the Blood Covenant.

[9] This idea is carried over and expressed in certain oaths by the words, *"The Lord do so to me, and more also, if I do not ...."* Examples of such oaths are found in I Samuel 3:17; 14:44; II Samuel 3:9, 35.

they would walk between the pieces of the animals and repeat the conditions of the covenant. In the case before us, Abraham saw what was taking place but did not participate. God alone entered into the covenant with His servant. He recounted what would happen to Abraham's descendants, and confirmed by this solemn oath that they would indeed possess the land. *"And it came about when the sun had set that it was very dark, and look, there appeared a smoking oven and a flaming torch that passed between the pieces. On that day the Lord made a covenant with Abram"* (Genesis 15:17ff.). This covenant was irrevocable. It answered Abraham's question about the land by promising it to him. It even specified the boundaries.

Our God is a gracious God. He understands our frailty, and He meets us (as He did Abraham) and answers our specific needs. This He does to all whose hearts are wholly committed to Him.

## INTERACTION

1. By consulting a good Bible dictionary, check such articles as "Barren, Barrenness," "Child, Children," and "Marriage." Find out all you can about the laws of inheritance. What is meant by *a "double portion"*?

2. It was said of Caleb that he *"wholly followed the Lord his God"* (cf. Numbers 14:24; 32:12; Deuteronomy 1:36; Joshua 14:8-14. Contrast Numbers 32:11). What can be learned from his example?

3. Read over Genesis 15:1-16:16 and take note of other cultural phenomena not covered in this chapter. Research each one in your Bible dictionary.

Chapter Eight

# AT THE CENTER

## THE DOCTRINAL METHOD

The study of theology[1] (or doctrine) comes from two Greek words, *Theos* ("God") and *logos* ("word, statement"). A study of "God," however, is beyond human comprehension, for no one can fully know God, and so no one can adequately explain Him and His ways. A knowledge of God forever lies outside the realm of our understanding except for the fact that He has chosen to reveal Himself in His Word, and we betray our infidelity to the truth if we do not seek out and master what He has chosen to reveal to us. To ignore such a primary resource is to leave ourselves adrift on a limitless sea of meaningless speculation, superstition, and uncertainty.

Theology has appropriately been called the "queen of the sciences." As such, our first efforts should be directed toward understanding it. Unfortunately, theology has

---

[1] Theology may be defined as that which is thought and said about God. Each religion and cult has its own idea(s). True doctrine is found in and founded upon the teaching of Scripture. It is the revelation of God in human terms. As such it is subject to exposition and reflection. It is this process that we engage in as we begin to uncover the teaching of the Bible on the person and work of God.

become contaminated by philosophy, with the result that it has also become the battleground of thinkers from the earliest times to the present. It is essential, however, if we are to discern correctly the strife between good and evil, that we possess more than a passing familiarity with what the Bible teaches. The more the adversary of our souls can obscure the truth, the easier it is for him to deceive those whom he wishes to destroy. The late Dr. Lewis Sperry Chafer wrote:

> Since doctrine is the bone and structure of revealed truth, the neglect of it must result in a message characterized by uncertainties, inaccuracies, and immaturity.... No substitute will ever be found for the Word of God.... There is a limitless yet hidden spiritual content within the Bible that contributes much to its supernatural character. This spiritual content is never discerned by the natural, or unregenerate man (I Corinthians 2:14), even though he has attained to the highest level of learning.[2]

## A WORTHY EXAMPLE

How then may we attain to a knowledge of the truth?

Numbered among the spiritual giants of all time is a man named Ezra. He was responsible for one of the most remarkable movements of the Spirit of God in all of

---

[2] L. S. Chafer, *Systematic Theology* (1947), I:v.

recorded history.[3] The spiritual teachers of his day had developed a dry orthodoxy that did not meet people's needs. Ezra determined not to perpetuate their tradition. Instead, he *"set his heart to study the law of the Lord, and to practice it, and to teach His statutes and ordinances in Israel"* (Ezra 7:10). He showed that theology has a practical side; and we, by following his three-fold approach, can explain our doctrine by our lives.

It should be our goal, therefore, to *study* the Word of God; put into *practice* what it teaches; and then *teach* others (cf. II Timothy 2:2). We should progress beyond an objective knowledge of the truth to a personal experience of it, and then communicate it effectively to those whom we meet.

## SOMETHING FOR EVERYONE

But what techniques can we use to investigate the different doctrines of the Bible? Where should we begin? What areas should we delve into?

Basically, there are three areas that we can research with the aid of our Bible and a concordance: (1) The main divisions of theology (e.g., God, Christ, the Holy Spirit, man, angels, salvation, the second coming, etc.); (2) the teaching of a specific writer (e.g., Moses, Paul, Luke, John); and selected topics (e.g., grace, love, forgiveness, fellowship, etc.). We will deal with these areas in

---

[3] See *Nehemiah and the Dynamics of Effective Leadership*, 121-47.

sequence. Gathering data about them follows the same methodology used previously, namely, *collecting, arranging, comparing, exhibiting,* and *defending* the material we have uncovered.

## *Return to Basics*

The first method—that follows the main divisions of Bible doctrine—is the most common. It gathers information under the traditional subject areas treated in most systems of theology:

- What the Bible records about itself.
- What the Bible teaches about the Godhead.
- What the Bible reveals about angels.
- What the Bible discloses about mankind.
- What the Bible unfolds about salvation.
- What the Bible tells us about the church.
- What the Bible unveils about the future.

*What the Bible records about itself.* Initially, we begin with what the Bible teaches about itself (often referred to as Bibliology). This is done, because, in our quest for truth, it is essential that we build upon a sure foundation. Bibliology includes such matters as inspiration,[4] revelation,[5] and other topics like inerrancy, authority, how we

---

[4] Defined as "God's superintending of human authors so that using their own individual personalities they composed and recorded without error His revelation to mankind in the words of the original autographs" (cf. II Timothy 3:16; II Peter 1:21; etc.).

[5] I.e., "Revelation is that act of God by which He communicates directly to the human mind that which was unknown

know which books belong in the Bible (called "canonicity"), and the laws governing interpretation.[6]

*What the Bible teaches about the Godhead.* A knowledge of the way God communicated information to us (i.e., through the Bible) is generally followed by a gathering of data about God Himself. There is only one God who exists in three persons—the Father, the Son, and the Holy Spirit. In the unity of the Godhead, each Member is eternal and coequal, the same in substance but distinct in subsistence. Intriguing facets of our study of the person of God center around a consideration of His attributes and also the significance of His names (e.g., LORD, *"Yahweh;"* God, *"El* or *Elohim;"* Lord, *Adonai*; and then compound forms of His names like "Lord of Hosts" or "God Most High," etc.).[7]

Because a study of what the Bible teaches about the Lord Jesus Christ (Christology)[8] and the Holy Spirit

---

before." This is done through nature (Romans 1:18-21; Psalm 19); providential dealings (Romans 8:28); preservation of the universe (Colossians 1:17); miracles (John 2:11; etc.); direct communication (Acts 22:17-21); the person and work of Christ (John 1:14; Hebrews 1:1-3); and through the teaching of Scripture (I John 5:9-12).

[6] These issues have been treated most adequately in the book by N. L. Geisler and W. E. Nix, *A General Introduction to the Bible* (1986), 724pp.

[7] Two excellent treatments of Bible doctrine are by P. P. Enns, *The Moody Handbook of Theology* (1989), 688pp., and the work by C. C. Ryrie, *Basic Theology* (1986), 544pp.

[8] A recent, highly commendable work is by J. A. Witmer, *Immanuel: Jesus Christ, Cornerstone of Our Faith* (1998), 199pp.

(Pneumatology)[9] is so extensive, these areas are often treated as separate subjects.

*What the Bible reveals about angels.* A consideration of created angelic beings (angelology) includes both good and bad (or fallen) angels and, of course, Satan. It focuses on their origin, order, ministry, and destiny.[10]

*What the Bible discloses about mankind.* Next comes the doctrine of man (anthropology) and this investigation is closely linked with the need for salvation (or, to use the theological term, soteriology[11]). Specific attention is given to man's origin, nature, present state, need for redemption, and future hope. Included in this division is the origin of sin, and its effects on and transmission into the human race. Of essential significance is the application of Christ's death to us. The doctrine of the atonement, by which Christ's blood becomes the basis of our salvation,[12] is foundational to an understanding of salvation.

*What the Bible tells us about the church.* Believers who have been saved by trusting Christ become part of a

---

[9] Able discussions include J. F. Walvoord's *The Holy Spirit* (1965), 288pp., and C. C. Ryrie's monograph *The Holy Spirit* (1965), 126pp.

[10] Additional, balanced information can be obtained from R. P. Lightner's *Angels, Satan and Demons* (1998), 212pp.

[11] E. D. Rademacher, *Salvation* (2000), 302pp.

[12] This aspect of theology has been discussed by Robert A. Pyne in *Humanity and Sin* (1999), 309pp.

new community, the Church[13] (hence, the study of ecclesiology). In this division it is customary to consider the origin and nature of the body of Christ, and the place of worship, exhortation, and instruction. Also within this area of theology, emphasis is placed on the unity, order, ordinances, and service of those who comprise the church.

*What the Bible unveils about the future.* Finally, there is the doctrine of "last things" (called eschatology). This topic includes God's plan and purpose for His people of different ages, as well as a discussion of death, immortality, the judgment that comes upon the unsaved and the rewards that are given the saved, the tribulation, the establishment of Christ's Kingdom, and the eternal state.[14]

As you can see, the range of theology (or Bible doctrine) is very broad. In fact, it embodies all that God has chosen to reveal to us and spans the gap between eternity past and eternity future.

## *Promising Results*

The second method of doctrinal Bible study is much simpler. It too involves gathering information, this time by means of a concordance. Our focus now is on the writings of a specific author (e.g., Moses, David, Luke, John or Paul) or teacher (e.g., Jesus Christ). By studying the

---

[13] The best and most reliable one-volume work on this subject is R. L. Saucy's *The Church in God's Program* (1972), 254pp.

[14] Innumerable books have been written in this area. Of significant value is J. F. Walvoord's *Major Bible Prophecies* (1991), 450pp.

writings of an author, we can uncover the doctrines that God chose to reveal to us through that person. For example, by working progressively through Genesis→Deuteronomy (and including Psalm 90 and other references to Moses), we can uncover the central idea around which themes in his writings revolve.

The same procedure can be followed with the writings of David. He is reputed to have written seventy-three psalms (with other anonymous ones believed to have come from his pen. And then there is information about him contained elsewhere in Scripture). All this forms a fruitful area of study, and leads us to understand more fully the kind of relationship David had with the Lord. Of course, each psalm must be considered in light of its historic background (often derived from the superscription), with information also being deduced from specific references in the text. We can then group together common themes and study them so as to ascertain how one builds upon another.

## *Developing Ideas*

The third method of doctrinal study is the one most frequently resorted to. It is oriented toward subjects. This approach likewise uses a concordance (though a good Bible dictionary may also be helpful). It scans the biblical text for relevant material that focuses on topics like praise, confession, forgiveness, grace, home and family, husband and father, wife and mother, law, love, maturity, parent-child relationships (especially in Proverbs 1-9), prayer, repentance, rewards, sex, sin, stewardship, and many more.[15]

---

[15] Excellent examples of this approach, each illustrating a different approach, include L. S. Chafer, *Major Bible Themes*, revised

## BLESSINGS IN DISGUISE

Whenever we engage in the study of Bible doctrine, it is important to keep in mind the fact that God's revelation is progressive. He did not "dump" an entire curriculum on us at the moment of our conversion. Abraham, for example, did not know all that we know about salvation, even though he knew experientially what it was like to be justified by faith (Romans 4). He knew the broad outline of the Abrahamic Covenant, and each time God appeared to him his understanding of the extent of God's promise was enlarged. He did not know about future additions to the basic covenant God had made with him (like the Palestinian, Davidic, and New Covenants). He had some knowledge of the second person of the Trinity, even though it was many centuries before the Lord Jesus was born (cf. John 8:56). He also knew the blessings of salvation and a life of faith (cf. Galatians 3:8; James 2:21, 23), experienced personal revelation from God (Genesis 12:1-3; 13:14ff.), and grew spiritually through obedience to the revealed will of God. Abraham also came progressively to understand more of God's nature through the revelation of His names. On the basis of Hebrews 11:9-10 it seems as if he were absolutely convinced of the bodily resurrection of the dead, and of a time still to come when he would personally

---

by J. F. Walvoord (1974), 374pp.; L. O. Richards, *Expository Dictionary of Bible Words* (1985), 720pp.; and W. E. Vine's *Complete Expository Dictionary of Old and New Testament Words* (1985), 755pp. (that includes *Nelson's Expository Dictionary of the Old Testament* by M. F. Unger and W. White).

inherit the land that God had promised to give him (compare Hebrews 11:3 and Revelation 21:2, 10-24).

How much Abraham understood of the full teaching of his "seed" (cf. Galatians 3:16), including the kings that would come from his line and of the birth of the Savior, is difficult to determine. He obviously believed that he would have numerous physical descendants (Isaiah 41:8), and possibly he could distinguish between those who would share his faith and those who would not (see Luke 3:8; John 8:39, 42, 63-59; Romans 9:6-8). He also knew that one day his "seed" would include Gentiles (Romans 4:16; Galatians 3:8-9) and that his ultimate Seed (Galatians 3:16), Christ, would rule over the nations of the earth.

We would not believe that all of this was possible were it not for the teaching of the Bible. The kind of knowledge that Abraham, the father of the faithful, possessed should be cherished by each one of us.

## THE COVENANT RENEWED

We, as believers, often find ourselves experiencing tension between God's promise and our personal experience. God's promise is clear; we may have prayed earnestly about the matter, claimed His promise, and yet our circumstances are the antithesis of our expectations. Abraham knew what this was like. On an earlier occasion he asked the Lord for a son, and God promised him innumerable descendants. But where were they? Time had passed, and Sarah had not borne him a son.

In Genesis 17, the Lord again comes to Abraham. The patriarch is now ninety-nine years old. Thirteen years have passed since the birth of Ishmael. On this occasion, the Lord reveals himself to Abraham as *El Shaddai*, *"God Almighty"* (Genesis 17:1-3). He talks with Abraham and reaffirms His covenant with him (Genesis 17:4-8). He also changes his name from *"Abram,"* *"exalted father,"* to *"Abraham"* *"father of a multitude."* He specifically tells Abraham that kings will be numbered in his line, and then reaffirms the fact that the land of Canaan is to be the possession of his descendants (Genesis 17:8). As confirmation of this, the Lord imposes the sign of circumcision (Romans 4:11).

Finally, the Lord speaks of Sarah (Genesis 17:15-21). He changes her name from *"Sarai"* to *"Sarah"* (meaning *"princess"*), and promises that Abraham will have a son by her (Genesis 17:16). He also identifies that the chosen line will be through Isaac, not Ishmael (Genesis 17:21).

Once again, we observe the Lord enlarging upon the specifics of the covenant made earlier with Abraham. None of the original conditions are changed. The covenant is reinforced and reaffirmed.

## INTERACTION

1. By far the most significant doctrine associated with Abraham's life is the Abrahamic Covenant. God promised to bless Abraham in three distinct areas: (1) national blessings that focused specifically on the land, (2) personal blessings that included a "seed," and (3) universal blessings. Begin

gathering data from Genesis 12:1-3; 13:14-18; 15:11-21; 17:1-27; 18:9-15, 17-19; and 22:9-19. Identify the specific area of the covenant mentioned in these verses. It may help you to do this in columns. Then summarize the teaching of these verses in succinct paragraphs.

2. Consider God's promise to Abraham (Genesis 13:14-15) and note the words *"to you."* Check Hebrews 11:8-10, 13. Will Abraham ever possess the land that God promised to give him? What does this indicate about God?

3. As you reread Genesis 17, note the attributes, descriptions, or characteristics of God. What does this tell us about Him? How does this contribute to the strengthening of our faith?

Chapter Nine

# ROOTS, RELATIONSHIPS AND RESPONSIBILITY

### THE SOCIOLOGICAL METHOD

Herman Wouk, who has given us such literary masterpieces as *The Caine Mutiny, The Winds of War,* and *War and Remembrance* (all of which were made into movies) also wrote a best seller entitled, *This Is My God.* In it he tells of a Jewish acquaintance, a skeptic, who one evening asked, "Can you recommend to me any good reading matter on Hanuka? I think my son should know a bit more about his Jewish background than he does." Then, realizing what was probably flashing through his famous friend's mind, he added wryly, "Purely for culture, you understand, not for religion!"[1]

This chance remark led Herman Wouk to write his apologetic for Judaism, for culture cannot be divorced from faith. If one's faith is mortgaged, then one's culture

---

[1] H. Wouk, *This Is My God,* (1959), 17.

becomes meaningless and the entire society of which one is a part is in danger of losing those very things that at one time contributed to its preservation.[2] Because the core of any society is the family, the things that affect the family are of paramount importance in the preservation of the society of which the family is a part.

In this chapter, we will focus primarily on Genesis 18:1-15 and 21:1-7. In an earlier chapter, we noted how the cultural method of Bible study includes everything that can be known about a given people—their arts and sciences, geographic location and history, literature and economy, religion and politics. Now, as we come to consider the cultural method, we can diagram our approach in a series of concentric circles. On the outer edge there is the nation; then moving inwards there is the tribe made up of families descended from a common ancestor; coming closer to the center there is the extended family which in Bible times was often very large and was made up of generations of sons with their wives and children; and finally, at the center, there is the inner circle—a single family made up of father, mother and children.

Obviously diverse influences were exerted on each tribe. The larger tribes enjoyed greater prominence, the smaller ones had less say in national affairs. Then there was the influence of the (extended) family. Were they rich and powerful? Were their lands extensive? How many servants did they have? Did any of their members *"sit at the gate"* and perform the duty of a judge? All of these factors would have a bearing on the family. The innermost

---

[2] This is the whole point of *Fiddler On the Roof*, where "culture = tradition."

circle involved the dyadic relationships of father-mother, parent-child, and each child to his or her siblings.

Because the family is the basic unit of all societies, and because the family invariably functions within the community (or society), it is appropriate to consider the environment in which the members of the family live, how they interact with one another, and the forces that regulate their lives. As we pursue this kind of inquiry, we will be surprised to find how much it contributes to our understanding of Scripture and the events about which we read. By concentrating our attention on the family unit, we will be able to find out different things about it (e.g., its size, location, structure, and relation to other families within the cultural circle).

In biblical times, the family tended to grow in size so that at one point it might consist of the patriarch, his wife (or wives), his sons, his son's wives, and their children. Take, for example, the family of Jacob as an illustration of growth. He had twelve sons. However, at the time they entered Egypt, they numbered nearly seventy individuals (Genesis 46:5-7, 26). Later, when they came out of Egypt under Moses, each family had become a tribe with its own leader and elders (Numbers 13:2-15; Exodus 4:29), and men over the age of twenty numbered six hundred thousand (Exodus 12:37-38). When wives and children are tallied, Jacob's family must have grown to approximately two million individuals. God constituted these tribes a nation at Mount Sinai, and gave them their own laws (Exodus 20-23).

While the organization of Abraham's "household" was fairly simple, later on in Israel's history, the social dynamics became more complicated. The challenge before us is to learn as much as we can about the community in which men and women of Bible times lived and worked, reared their children, sustained their faith in God, organized themselves, and maintained harmonious relationships with other members of their tribe.

## TIMELY TOPIC

In the passages before us (*viz.*, Genesis 18:1-15 and 21:1-7) we read ...

> *Now the Lord appeared to him [i.e., Abraham] by the oaks of Mamre, while he was sitting at the tent door in the heat of the day. When he lifted up his eyes and looked, behold, three men were standing opposite him; and when he saw them, he ran from the tent door to meet them and bowed himself to the earth, and said, "My lord, if now I have found favor in your sight, please do not pass your servant by. Please let a little water be brought and wash your feet, and rest yourselves under the tree; and I will bring a piece of bread, that you may refresh yourselves; after that you may go on, since you have visited your servant."*
> 
> *And they said, "So do, as you have said."*
> 
> *So Abraham hurried into the tent to Sarah, and said, "Quickly, prepare three measures of fine flour, knead it and make bread cakes." Abraham also ran to the herd, and took a tender and choice calf and gave it to the servant, and he hurried to*

*prepare it. He took curds and milk and the calf that he had prepared, and placed it before them; and he was standing by them under the tree as they ate.*

*Then they said to him, "Where is Sarah your wife?"*

*And he said, "There, in the tent."*

*He said, "I will surely return to you at this time next year; and behold, Sarah your wife will have a son."*

*And Sarah was listening at the tent door, which was behind him. Now Abraham and Sarah were old, advanced in age; Sarah was past childbearing. Sarah laughed to herself, saying, "After I have become old, shall I have pleasure, my lord being old also?"*

*And the Lord said to Abraham, "Why did Sarah laugh, saying, 'Shall I indeed bear a child, when I am so old?' Is anything too difficult for the Lord? At the appointed time I will return to you, at this time next year, and Sarah will have a son."*

*Sarah denied it however, saying, "I did not laugh"; for she was afraid. And He said, "No, but you did laugh...."*

*Then the Lord took note of Sarah as He had said, and the Lord did for Sarah as He had promised. So Sarah conceived and bore a son to Abraham in his old age, at the appointed time of which God had spoken to him. Abraham called the name of his son who was born to him, whom*

*Sarah bore to him, Isaac. Then Abraham circumcised his son Isaac when he was eight days old, as God had commanded him. Now Abraham was one hundred years old when his son Isaac was born to him.*

*Sarah said, "God has made laughter for me; everyone who hears will laugh with me." And she said, "Who would have said to Abraham that Sarah would nurse children? Yet I have borne him a son in his old age."*

In these verses, we have the opportunity to observe the family life of Abraham and Sarah. It is most instructive to read through and list under different headings items like "hospitality," "family relationships," "social attitudes" (toward servants, sex, possessions), "acts of kindness," et cetera. Once this has been done, the data can be analyzed and implications drawn from the text.

By way of illustration, let us take one of the main topics found in Genesis 18, namely, hospitality. We can enter "Hospitality" in our notebook and then begin to list all of the information that comes directly from our study of the text. In doing so, we can ask ourselves questions to prompt our thought processes: e.g., At what time of day did Abraham and Sarah have guests drop in on them unexpectedly? What was their reaction? Why did they respond as they did? How did they entertain them? What role(s) did each assume?

Your notebook might look something like this:

*Verses 1-2. Time: Midday. Siesta, too hot to work. Inconvenient. Attitude: Cordial. No resentment evident. Guests are treated with the utmost courtesy.*

*Verses 3-5. Kind invitation. Respectful. Invited to stay, refresh themselves by washing their feet. Offered " a morsel of bread." In reality, Abraham provides a satisfying meal.*
*Verses 6-8. The hurried preparations. Abraham and Sarah shared the duties. Sarah baked. Abraham ran to where some cattle were in a stall. Why the elaborate preparations?*
*Verse 8a. Why did Abraham serve the guests himself?*

And so you can go on. This preliminary investigation might call for a topical study of hospitality, using both your Bible dictionary and a Bible concordance. Each verse referenced in these resources should then be studied in its context and the implications noted under appropriate subheadings.

## HISTORIC HIGHLIGHTS

A second approach to the sociological method of Bible study focuses attention on the family structure. The primary family structures in the ancient Near East were patriarchal and matriarchal. In the Bible, they tended to be patriarchal. In our day, with the rise in the rate of divorce and with some people opting to have children without getting married, we now have to contend with single-parent families that are primarily matriarchal. From a biblical point of view, however, it was always God's intent for children to live with their father and mother. And in this respect the home of Abraham and Sarah provides a good model.

Considerable information about family relationships can be gleaned from the Book of Proverbs (chapters 1-9), from conversations in the Bible, or from the way in which certain duties were performed.

In the case of Abraham and Sarah, it appears that they were both sitting in the shade of their tent (which also enjoyed the shade of a tree [cf. 18:1, 6*a*, 8*b*, 10*b*]) during the siesta-time of the day. It seems probable that Abraham and Sarah raised the flap of their tent so as to benefit from whatever breeze might blow, and then spent the hot afternoons talking with each other, sharing their feelings, and describing their longings. In this, they set an example for couples today. Because of our fast-paced society many of us have forgotten how to communicate and over time have come to ignore this vital part of life.

As we continue our study, we might profitably inquire into Sarah's status. Was she a mere chattel, as some modern writers would have us believe, or did Abraham treat her with respect? Verses 6 and 7 supply a partial answer. When guests dropped in unexpectedly, Abraham extended to them the hospitality generally accorded visitors. He also felt free to ask Sarah to bake bread for them. Now let us remember that it was the heat of the day, and they had no microwave ovens or other modern conveniences. And Sarah, who had probably dropped the flaps of their tent as the men approached, made the cakes without complaint. But Abraham did not leave everything to Sarah. Though ninety-nine years old, he ran to the enclosure of thorn bushes where animals for their meals were kept, caught a young calf, and gave it to one of his servants to prepare for roasting. In this, we see that Abraham and Sarah shared responsibility for preparing the meal. They assumed different duties, but obviously enjoyed equality as persons. And we should not overlook the fact that, in serving their guests, Abraham stood[3] and waited on them himself.

All of these facts, gleaned from the biblical text, give us some indication of the sociology of the times.

In pursuing our study further, we should seek to determine the attitude of people within the family. For example, how comfortable was Abraham in his role as a man, and what was Sarah's attitude toward herself as a woman? At the bottom of these questions lies the way in which each viewed his or her sexual identity. When it became evident that one of Abraham's guests was the Second Person of the Trinity, Abraham was asked about Sarah. She was modestly inside the tent behind the flap that separated the men's quarters from those of the women.

When God promised that, at this time next year, Sarah would have a son, she laughed within herself and questioned, *"After I have become old, shall I have **pleasure**, my lord being old also?"* (Genesis 18:12*b*, emphasis added). Take note of the word "pleasure." In the original it is the word *ednah*, "sexual delight." People in the ancient Near East knew that sex was for pleasure, and not solely for reproduction. And it was not a subject that was considered too delicate for polite society. Sex for pleasure was considered a natural part of life.

Notice, too, Sarah's attitude. Without any inhibitions she refers to her uniform experience of sex as one of delight and satisfaction. Her words give no indication that she was a "sex object" and had been forced to submit to the

---

[3] Slaves or servants stood while their masters ate the meal.

boorish demands of her husband. The implication is clear. Within the bounds of marriage the tender intimacy of husband and wife was enjoyable, and Sarah gave no indication that she had ever been "used" by her husband.

## TOP PRIORITY

A third consideration in our study of the sociology of the family might well focus on the method of child-rearing. Notice what God said about Abraham: *"For I have chosen him,* ***so that he may command his children and his household after him to keep the way of the LORD by doing righteousness and justice,*** *so that the LORD may bring upon Abraham what He has spoken about him"* (Genesis 18:19, emphasis added).

These words provide (in broad outline) a pattern of socialization. The husband and father is to order the lives of those in his household so that they will *"keep the way of the Lord by doing righteousness and justice."* It is his wise leadership, consistent example, balanced judgment, and authoritative headship that is needed if children are to grow to maturity secure in themselves and able to relate with confidence to the world of which they are a part.

In Genesis 21, God's promise to Abraham and Sarah (made 25 years earlier) is realized. Sarah bears Abraham a son, and he calls his name "Isaac" meaning "laughter." Isaac is circumcised to show that he is identified with the Abrahamic Covenant (Genesis 17:9-14). Now notice Sarah's reaction. The social stigma she had borne for so long has been removed. Her attitude is now one of rejoicing. She says, *"God has made laughter for me;*

*everyone who hears will laugh with me.... I have borne [Abraham] a son in his old age"* (Genesis 21:6-7).

Isaac grew and was probably nursed by his mother for three years, and then weaned.

It was generally the custom for children in Bible times to follow the occupation of their parents. If a son's father was a shepherd, he would in all probability become a shepherd; if his father was a carpenter, he would probably become a carpenter (Matthew 13:55; Mark 6:3); if a son's father was a fisherman, he would probably become a fisherman (Matthew 4:21-22). This is of more than passing interest. A son spent a good deal of time with his father, and a father taught his son all he knew about life and his occupation. As a result, the beliefs and values of the father frequently became the beliefs and values of his son.

In like manner, daughters learned from their mothers how to cook, sew, weave, and perform different domestic duties. They were prepared for adulthood by their mothers and imbibed much of their attitude toward life in general and men in particular from their mothers.

## GROWTH OF GOD-CONSCIOUSNESS

So far in our consideration of the family life of Abraham and Sarah, we have looked at their hospitality, interpersonal relationships, sexual attitudes, and parental roles. It now becomes necessary to consider the growth of their spiritual lives.

Something about the "visitors" that came to Abraham and Sarah's camp impressed them, for Abraham offered them the finest delicacies of Oriental hospitality (Genesis 18:8). Only in verse 14 did the Lord identify Himself.

Abraham's faith grew with each new revelation. Sarah's faith also grew as a result of the things Abraham told her. But now, as the Lord conversed with Abraham, she listened from inside the tent and heard God promise that *she* would have a son (Genesis 18:9-15). At first she did not believe her ears. Her laughter was a mixture of incredulity (arising out of her knowledge of her present condition) and disappointment, for she had trusted in such a promise when she and Abraham had left Ur twenty-five years earlier. But when the Lord rebuked her unbelief, she became silent. She knew that only an omniscient God could have read her innermost thoughts. And, as we find in Hebrews 11:11, *"By faith even Sarah herself received ability to conceive, even beyond the proper time of life, since she considered Him faithful who had promised [her a son]."*

Not only were God's words to Sarah personal, but they reminded her (and all generations since), that there is nothing too hard for the Lord. He performed what He had promised, and through the process Sarah grew in spiritual awareness of His power and personal interest in her.

## HELP ... I'M HUMAN

Of course, much more could be said of the sociological method of Bible study. We could examine in detail the effect of heredity and environment upon children, the rights of the firstborn, and the respect to be paid the aged. The Book of Genesis provides ample information for such a study, as well as the application of specific principles to modern marital situations.[4] Our present interest in the subject has been limited to specific incidents in the life of Abraham and Sarah. The practical application of these truths should not be ignored. And, as the great Bible expositor, Dr. W. H. Griffith Thomas, has pointed out "Abraham illustrates the opportunity for men and women of faith to enjoy sacred intimacy with God" (Genesis 18:2-5; Hebrews 13:1-2).[5] Dr. Thomas also demonstrated the need for "genuine humility" (Genesis 18:6-8) and shows how this paved the way for "special revelation" (Genesis 18:9-15).[6] Through the fulfillment of God's promise to Abraham and Sarah, we learn of the unchanging faithfulness of God (Genesis 21:1-7), for the Lord did *"exactly as He had spoken."* We also see the perfect wisdom of God (Genesis 21:8ff.), for God shows that He is able to accomplish His purpose for us in spite of previous failure and unbelief. Furthermore, from this point onward Abraham and Sarah's joy bore testimony to the absolute sufficiency of God, for He was able to meet their needs.

Sarah enjoyed Isaac's companionship for thirty-seven years (Genesis 17:17; 23:1), and both she and Abraham must have felt that God more than compensated them for their long wait for the child of promise to be born.

---

[4] Two books that deal specifically with marriages in the Bible and apply what is learned from them to modern relationships are *Your Marriage Has Real Possibilities* (1990), 221pp., and *Your Marriage Can Last a Lifetime* (1989), 190pp.

[5] Thomas, *Genesis*, 161.

[6] *Ibid.*, 187.

God doesn't change. He is able, even today, to do exceeding abundantly above all that we could ever ask or think. Let us therefore learn of Him as Abraham and Sarah did, order our lives according to His Word, and wait patiently for His promises to be fulfilled.

## INTERACTION

Check your Bible dictionary under "Food," and search out the staples of the working class and the delicacies of the affluent. When did people in Bible times eat the main meal of the day? Of what did this meal consist? How were meats, fruits, et cetera, prepared and preserved? What specific instructions did God give the Israelites in order to insure their continued good health? How would a visitor feel toward his host if served "curds and milk"? How frequently did people in Bible times eat beef?

What was the effect of parental involvement on a young child, boy or girl, as he/she was growing toward adulthood? What may be gleaned from a consideration of Genesis 18:19 and the way in which Abraham must have reared Ishmael and later Isaac? What occupation did each follow (cf. Genesis 13:2 with 26:14; contrast 21:20)?

Make a chart by paragraphs of Genesis 18-21 and note specifics that enlarge our understanding of the family life of Abraham and Sarah.

Chapter Ten

# LEARNING ABOUT PEOPLE

## THE BIOGRAPHICAL METHOD

### Part 1

God is interested in people. Proof of this may be seen in the large portions of the Bible that are devoted to stories about people. Human biographers are inclined to err in either maximizing the better qualities of their subjects and minimizing their weaknesses, or else diminishing the worth and contribution of a person with the result that they rob a rising generation of their heroes. The Bible, however, presents people accurately and without veneer. And in the process they are shown to possess a nature like our own (cf. James 5:17).

Several years ago, when I annually taught a course in "Spiritual Growth" at the Rosemead Graduate School of Psychology, I would assign my students the task of writing on a Bible character of their choice. On one occasion, a student openly challenged the assignment. His anger was ill-concealed. He stated bluntly that he could not do the assignment because he could not administer any psychological tests to the person about whom he felt compelled to write. Such an approach is tragic. It manifests at least two weaknesses. It totally misunderstands the nature of Bible biography, and naively places greater reliance on psychological tests than it does on the Spirit of God who guides us into all truth.

The usual approach to biographies is to study a person's life from his or her birth to his/her death and, along the way, assess the major influences of his or her life before describing his/her contribution to society. Bible biographies are different. They are more like sketches. In our study of them it is important for us to notice the prominence given by the original writers to an individual's actions and words. *No detail is unimportant.* Dr. G. N. Stanton, in his *Jesus of Nazareth in New Testament Preaching,* points out that in the Bible a person's life is explained succinctly through his words and actions. "[So it is that] a phrase or jest often makes a greater revelation of character than battles [won or lost] ...."[1] This point had been made much earlier by Dr. John Howson in his fine work, *The Companions of St. Paul*:

> No religious book is less symmetrical than the Bible in its arrangement of doctrines and precepts; yet in no book is there so complete a code of faith and duty for all the varied circumstances of life.... In whatever condition we may be placed, light and guidance is always provided for us in the pages of Scripture.... *Sometimes through the indirect teaching of an example, sometimes through words dropped incidentally ... sometimes by the revelation of causal circumstances, which*

---

[1] G. N. Stanton, *Jesus of Nazareth in New Testament Preaching* (1974), 117.

*unexpectedly reveal great truths*; it is thus ... that we learn to **"understand what the will of the Lord is."** *Hence the full benefit of Scripture is not to be got except by patient search and close comparison. The careless reader misses much. The diligent and well-equipped student is often surprised when he finds how parts of the Bible, which seemed intended for no such purpose, are* **"profitable for doctrine, for reproof, for correction, for instruction in righteousness."**[2]

## WHERE TO BEGIN

With these thoughts in mind, we are now about to embark on an exciting adventure—one that will last you the rest of your life! As you begin, you will need to do three things:

- Collect all pertinent facts about the person whose life you are studying.
- Carefully analyze and interpret these facts as they relate to his/her life.
- Compare these facts with information available from other sources.

In the collection of data, the best place to start is with a concordance. Look up the individual's name and locate all the passages in the Bible that mention him or her. This

---

[2] J. S. Howson, *The Companions of St. Paul* (n.d.), 178-79. He shares similar, pertinent insights in his Introduction. All are worth noting.

done, the next task is to read through these passages and determine from the context the precise value of the information being presented. Someone like Moses or David, Ruth or Esther, Peter or Paul has an enormous amount written about them, whereas other individuals like Deborah or Hannah, Mary or Silas have relatively little recorded of them. In addition, historical and doctrinal, spiritual and cultural details will need to be studied in light of the context of each passage. For our purpose, we will study Abraham's nephew, Lot.

We find information about Lot scattered throughout Genesis, Deuteronomy, the Psalms, the gospel of Luke, and II Peter. (References to Lot's descendants, unless they cast light on his character, may be subordinated to a secondary category.) The passages under consideration reveal Lot in different roles: (1) As an orphan, (2) as a cattle rancher, (3) as a captive, and (4) as a judge. Each vignette is separated from the others by a lapse of time, and each is permeated with important cultural and historical information.

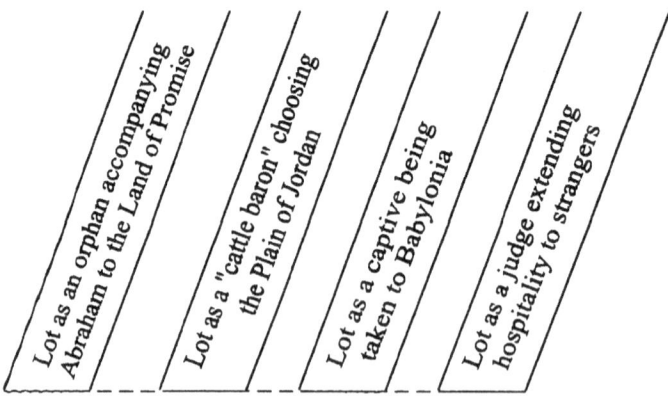

As we weigh each circumstance, we see Lot facing certain crises. While living in Ur his father dies, and Lot is taken into his grandfather's home (Genesis 11:27, 31); Lot suffers a further sense of loss when the family (under the leadership of his grandfather, Terah) moves from the populous city of Ur to the dirty caravan town of Haran; then Terah dies. In all probability, Lot becomes the "ward" of his childless uncle, Abraham, and his aunt, Sarah (who probably need him to complete their family circle as much as he needs them for security).

As we continue our study of Lot's life, we take note of the fact that twice the biblical record mentions the fact that when Abraham moved from one place to another, *"Lot went with him"* (Genesis 12:4; 13:1). But how does this enlarge upon our understanding of the motivating factors in his life?

It is probable that, as a young man, Lot inherited his father's estate. He became wealthy overnight. Had he so desired, he could have stayed in Ur ... or Haran. Instead, he chose to accompany Abraham on his pilgrimage of faith. And in time, they came to Canaan. Does this indicate personal faith in the God whom Abraham worshipped? Certainly, each time Abraham built an altar to the Lord, Lot saw it; and in the quiet of evenings spent around the campfire, he had ample opportunity to question his uncle about his personal faith in an unseen God. But such theorizing without proof can only be categorized as speculation, and so we must ask, "Is there any irrefutable evidence that Lot came to faith in Abraham's God?"

In II Peter 2:7, we are specifically told that Lot was a righteous man, and his decision to accompany Abraham to Canaan would seem to indicate something of his beliefs and values.[3] But intermingled with his spiritual commitment might also have been an emotional one—he could not bear the thought of further loss, and Abraham represented a degree of security. And so, possibly in the idealism of young manhood, and possibly not realizing fully how his own personality dynamics were interwoven in his decision, he decided to accompany Abraham to Canaan.

After a brief settlement in the Negev, Abraham moved down to Egypt. And Lot must have accompanied him, for later he returned with Abraham to Bethel (Genesis 13:1). In Egypt, Lot must have witnessed his uncle's plan to deceive Pharaoh. If Lot had idolized his uncle (as young people often do), he may have received a rude awakening when Abraham was expelled from Egypt. If so, he learned the bitter lesson that all our heroes have feet of clay. Even in the parenting process, this is true. Our children will find some flaw and, no matter how small it may be, it often becomes the ground for their rejection of us and our ideals. Of course, this is part of their growth toward maturity and

---

[3] Our beliefs are related to our values. The first level of belief is at the *acceptance* level. This is the level of mental activity. It involves the mind and implies "belief" in certain theories, facts, and ideals. The missing ingredient is trust. James 2:19 indicates that conversion does not take place at this level. The second level is the one at which *preference* is evident. At this level the mind and the emotions work in harmony and motivate the will to take appropriate action. This is the level of our being at which conversion takes place. In the case of Lot, Peter informs us that he was a "righteous man," and his preference can be seen in his accompanying Abraham to the land God had promised to give him. The final level of belief is the *commitment* level. At this level truths are valued to such an extent that a person gives himself/herself entirely to them. This is the level at which progressive sanctification begins.

the exercise of their independence, but those of us who have parented adolescents wish it weren't so traumatic.

In the course of time, Lot may have grown tired of being regarded as the orphaned nephew of the great sheik (Genesis 12:5). Perhaps he desired to be thought of as a wealthy man (a sheik) in his own right (Genesis 14:12). Whatever Lot's inner thoughts may have been, the biblical text mentions only that the hilly, rock-strewn area between Bethel and Ai was inadequate for the livestock of both men. Their herdsmen began to argue and fight among themselves.

When this came to Abraham's attention, he offered his nephew a choice. *"Please let there be no strife between you and me, nor between your herdsmen and my herdsmen, for we are brothers (i.e., kinfolk). Is not the whole land before you? Please separate from me: If to the left, then I will go to the right; or if to the right, then I will go to the left"* (Genesis 13:8-9). And Lot, we are told, chose the well-watered valley of the River Jordan (Genesis 13:11).

Abraham's offer causes us to question whether Abraham and Sarah were in the habit of indulging their nephew. And was Lot accustomed to having the best of everything? At no time did he defer to his uncle. He may have been spoiled because he was an orphan; and he had most assuredly grown to manhood accustomed to the benefits of inherited wealth; but does this excuse the selfishness of his choice? And why did he choose to journey so far away from his aunt and uncle that contact with them was virtually lost?

Whatever Lot's reasons, he seems to have lacked the same strong internal Godward orientation that Abraham had, for he chose according to what his eyes saw and what his heart desired, and not according to what he might have discerned on closer inspection. Eventually, he moved into the city of Sodom itself. Then the Bible adds the solemn statement: *"Now the men of Sodom were wicked exceedingly and sinners against the Lord"* (Genesis 13:13).

## THE STUDY OF CHARACTER

Leaving Lot for the moment, let us review the specifics that can be applied to the biographical method of Bible study. There are certain universal truths that apply to all people, and there are certain special criteria that apply only to the individual we are studying.

**Universal Truths.** Adam and Eve, from whom we are all descended, were created in the image of God. This means that He gave them certain of His attributes. They were uniquely gifted with an intellect (mind), sensibilities (emotions), and volition (a will) that were untarnished by sin (Genesis 1:26-27). Their intellect enabled them to recognize the truth and build their store of knowledge; their sensibilities provided a basis for them to exercise love, seek holiness and (in time) administer justice; and their wills gave them freedom and power so that they could respond to clear signals from the interplay of their minds and their emotions.

God also planted a beautiful garden and placed the first couple in it (Genesis 2:8). *Adam and Eve drew their identity from God and enjoyed unclouded fellowship with Him.*

## Learning About People 151

After Adam and Eve had enjoyed their garden-home for some time, they succumbed to temptation. Sin entered the world. Instead of their lives being God-centered, their thoughts now turned away from Him and they became self-centered.[4] Their *minds* were darkened, so that they could no longer perceive the issues clearly (cf. Romans 1:21; Ephesians 4:18). Their *emotions* were deadened, and they could no longer love God as He deserved (cf. Ephesians 2:1, 5; Colossians 2:13). And because their individual *wills* still received input from their minds and emotions, their wills no longer responded in obedience to God. And Adam and Eve, becoming conscious of effects of sin for the first time in their lives, hid from Him.[5]

We all share in these tragic effects brought about by sin's entrance into the world. Theologians call this event "the Fall." The result is that some of us try to think our way through the different situations of life with our minds controlling our actions. We tend to be compulsive and may even deny our true feelings. If something appears right, we

---

[4] Many psychologists, following a humanistic philosophy, have perpetuated man's self-centeredness by referring in their writings to mankind's basic *self*-worth, quest for *self*-esteem, desire for *self*-improvement, and the process of *self*-actualization, etc. They ignore the fact that now, as with Adam and Eve, the only truly healthy personality is the one that draws its identify from a vertical relationship with God, and not solely from our horizontal relationships (as rewarding as some of these may be).

[5] In Psalm 104:2 we are told that God covers Himself with light as with a garment. There are those who believe that a *"garment of light"* was part of the image and likeness of God that He gave to Adam and Eve at the time of creation. If this is so, it would explain how, as the light that emanated from their bodies began to fade, they became aware of the fact that they were naked.

do it. The input we give our wills is fairly predictable. We are often insensitive to the feelings of others, but excuse ourselves for any brusqueness because we see things in black and white.

Other people, however, are the very opposite. They are emotionally oriented. They live by the way they feel. Logic plays little part in their lives. The input they give their wills is such that their personal desires frequently override their reason.

Why? Sin has adversely affected the way we function. In light of this it is interesting to evaluate Lot's choices.

The Bible states that the process of restoration is through the Holy Spirit working within us and using the Word of God to enlighten our darkened minds (Romans 12:2; Ephesians 4:23). When the truth is perceived and accepted, the mind provides positive instruction that the emotions can recognize as right and respond to appropriately. Then, with the mind and emotions working together, they can give balanced directives to the will.

But there's more. Our choices are affected by our sense of security. Something else happened to Adam and Eve when they sinned, and it has a bearing on you and me today. While in Eden, our first parents enjoyed a unique situation. They were secure in every respect. They were the special objects of God's love and care. They lived in the perfect environment that God had created for them. This gave them a feeling of *belonging*. They were also the apex of God's creative handiwork, and God met with them in the cool of the evening and fellowshipped with them. This gave them a sensation of *worth*. God had also given them work to do, and because the environment was benign, they could easily accomplish His will. This gave them an awareness of their *competence*.[6]

When sin entered the world, all of this was changed. They felt alienated from God and were soon thrust out of the Garden. The ground was cursed and they now had to work hard to eke out an existence. They had lost everything that made them feel loved and wanted. Now they felt only loneliness and insecurity. And this they bequeathed to their children.

How does all of this have a bearing on the life of Lot? Lot's early life did not contribute to feelings of security. The death of his father must have caused him to feel lonely and insecure. To be sure, he was taken into the home of his grandfather, but when he too died, Lot became the "ward" of his uncle, Abraham. In the presence of Abraham, he enjoyed a sense of well-being. As he grew older, he probably began to experience an inner conflict. He probably wanted to exercise his independence, but each time he thought of something, he needed to clear it with his uncle.

The solution, he believed, was to move away. But when he moved away, his old insecurities caused him to make one unwise choice after another. He felt vulnerable out on the plain of the River Jordan. If he had not known this before, he soon learned that Bedouin bands loved to raid unsuspecting encampments, rape and pillage, and drive off the livestock. As this weighed more and more on Lot's mind, he decided to move closer to Sodom. Then, as his

---

[6] This information has been enlarged upon in the book by C. J. Barber and G. H. Strauss entitled *Leadership: The Dynamics of Success* (1982), 25-103.

fears persisted, he believed he would be more secure within a city with stout walls to protect it. And so, in spite of any misgivings he may have had, he moved into Sodom. And he prospered; but as the Apostle Peter pointed out, he was not happy. The evil conduct of the Sodomites vexed his righteous soul from day to day (II Peter 2:7-8), and because *"evil companions corrupt good manners"* (I Corinthians 15:33), it took its toll on his Godward relationship.

All of this compels us to take a closer look at our insecurities. The security that Adam and Eve forfeited can only be restored through a vital Godward relationship. Abraham knew the reality of fellowship with God and the sense of *belonging* that such fellowship provided. He did not need the security of a city for his peace and comfort. Furthermore, through the provisions of the Abrahamic Covenant he also came progressively to know his *worth*. And while not possessing all that the covenant promised him, his faith gave him *confidence*.

Real security for you and me comes to us in the same way. The New Testament enlarges upon the teaching of the Old Testament and shows how we, through a vital relationship with God the Father, can enjoy a sense of *belonging*. Through the new birth we are made members of His family (I John 3:1-2). We have access into His presence (Romans 5:1-2), and we are assured that nothing can separate us from His love (Romans 8:28-39; Hebrews 13:5-6).[7] But this is not all. Through an intimate

---

[7] It is interesting to note that in the Greek text of Hebrews 13:5 there are five negatives emphasizing as strongly as possible the fact that (to quote the hymn writer) "He will never, no never, no never depart" from the believer.

relationship with the Lord Jesus Christ, we are given a new sense of *worth*. We have been redeemed with a price far exceeding anything that the world could offer (I Peter 1:18-19), and we have been made heirs with Him in His Kingdom (Romans 8:17; Galatians 4:4-7). Lastly, through the indwelling of the Holy Spirit we are empowered for every task (John 14:12; II Corinthians 2:14-3:6). He is the source of our *competence*.

*Our Basic Needs.* But what motivates us to make certain decisions (even as Lot did) and do the things we do? Motivation, we are told, can be structured according to a hierarchy of needs.[8] It is like a pyramid. At the bottom of this pyramid are our physiological needs (i.e., freedom from hunger, thirst, and our need for air to breathe); these are followed by our safety needs (i.e., freedom from the threat of danger, and the need to ally ourselves with the familiar and the secure); after this comes our belonging and love needs (also called "affiliation and acceptance needs," that include the desire to feel loved and to love in return); then come our esteem needs (i.e., the desire for achievement, strength, reputation, status, prestige); these, in turn, are followed by actualization needs (i.e., the desire for fulfillment, the realization of our potential); and finally, there are our cognitive needs—the desire to understand, to satisfy our curiosity, to tackle the unknown.

Choices—Lot's or yours or mine—are often based upon our perception of our needs. We are guided in our choices by the self-centered desires of our fallen, sinful

---

[8] See A. Maslow's *Motivation and Personality* (1970). Though not a Christian, Maslow does provide a useful format for assessing our personal choices.

human understanding. Unaided by God, it is hard to choose what is right!

Lot's growth needs and desire for esteem (i.e., to be considered a person of importance and not always to have to stand in Abraham's shadow) led him to choose the well-watered valley of the Jordan (Genesis 13:10-11). As soon as he moved down into the valley, however, he felt vulnerable. He was no longer under the protective aegis of his powerful uncle. To make up for this lack and to ally himself with the familiar and the secure (such as he had known in Ur), he moved first near to Sodom and finally settled in it.

With these needs met, we find Lot's desires for love and affection surfacing. He married a woman of Sodom and reared a family in that city (Genesis 19:1-26). And with these needs taken care of, we next find his desire for status being satisfied when he sought the office of a judge (Genesis 19:1).[9]

Unfortunately for Lot, these externals never brought him peace and contentment. He lacked the spiritual enlightenment and satisfaction that Abraham enjoyed, and he never reached a higher level of growth where he felt fulfilled and at peace within himself. As such, Lot stands out on the pages of Scripture as the prototype of many people today who spend their lives trying through human means to meet and satisfy their essentially spiritual needs.

## INTERACTION

1. Imagine that Lot's wife has come to you for help. Her complaint centers in her husband. She is devoted to him, but after ten years of marriage has come to the conclusion that they are "incompatible." Differences that before were not apparent now seem to be increasingly important to both of them. Although Lot is a good husband, and his care of their girls is all that a mother could ask for, nothing seems to satisfy him. Inwardly he is restless. He lacks trust in his employees. He has been very successful, but fears that his very success will draw him to the attention of some Bedouin band that will come one night and steal his flocks and herds. And when he is not worrying about his livestock, he is fretting over the possibility that this year's profits may not be as large as last year's, or that his political enemies in Sodom may undermine his plans or plot his downfall. Mrs. Lot has done everything in her power to make her husband feel loved, but to no avail. She says ruefully, "Lot appears, at least outwardly, to have everything a man could wish for, but inwardly he gives me the impression that he is unsure of himself and so is prone to depression." What counsel would you give her?
2. Discuss with a friend, or with your Bible study partner or group, the effect of our minds and our

---

9     See Davis, Paradise to Prison, 200.

wills on the decisions we all must make. What additional light does Scripture shed on the process?
3. Feelings of belonging, worth, and competence are essential to our happiness. How may God's provision for us be appropriated and made a part of our everyday experience?

Chapter Eleven

# LEARNING ABOUT PEOPLE

## THE BIOGRAPHICAL METHOD

### Part 2

The Bible is unique among the world's religious literature. Its message, when acted upon, invests life with significance, and in the process, its truth brings the light of understanding to our darkened minds.

The Bible is also filled with factual information about people and their problems. It treats their emotions candidly, and illustrates how each need or desire may be handled. Abraham, as we have seen, following his defeat of Chedorlaomer, knew the gnawing pain of anxiety and apprehension (Genesis 15:1); Moses became frustrated with the intransigence of the Israelites and gave way to a fit of anger (Numbers 20:9-11); Samuel, after long years of faithful service to the nation, felt the sting of rejection (I Samuel 8); Joseph, as a result of the jealousy of his brothers and the scorn of Potiphar's wife, experienced injustice upon injustice (Genesis 37:27-28; 39:10-18); Mark, after having accompanied Paul and Barnabas on their missionary journey, felt the burning coals of humiliation brought on by failure (Acts 13:13); Paul was burdened with the care of the churches (II Corinthians 11:28); and John bore patiently the trials brought on by enforced separation from those whom he loved (Revelation 1:9). Through a study of Bible personalities, we learn about people and the way in which they handled their problems or used their resources.

In our previous chapter, we began discussing the elements of personality and, from a consideration of the life of Lot, found that the biblical data presents him in four different ways: (1) As an orphan, (2) as a "cattle baron," (3) as a captive, and (4) as a judge. On closer examination, we took note of the choices he made, and probed the possible reason for his decisions. Perhaps the strangest choice of all was his return to live in Sodom after Chedorlaomer's conquest and his rescue by Abraham.

We also assessed whether or not a basic hierarchy of needs fitted Lot's particular circumstances, and found that he was willing to compromise with evil in order to satisfy his longings. What he desired was not always wrong, though his motivation was selfish and he left God out of his life.

## LESSONS NOT LEARNED

Looking back to Genesis 14 and the record of the attack of the kings of the East, we are reminded of the fact that Chedorlaomer and his allies looted the cities on the east side of the River Jordan, completely destroying everything they could not carry away. Then, they turned westward toward Edom before turning northward so as to attack Sodom and Gomorrah. As we found when we studied that chapter, Lot, together with the people of the cities at the southern end of the Dead Sea, was taken captive. Everything he (and they) possessed was regarded by the victors as the legitimate spoils of war. What were

## Learning About People 161

Lot's feelings as he was led away?[1] Chedorlaomer and those with him had deprived him of his autonomy and they had the power to sell him into slavery.[2] Did he think of his uncle, Abraham, who was living in perfect safety, although only a few miles away?

The text does not go into specifics as to how Lot felt, but it is not hard to imagine his anguish. His comfort zone had been breached. Fear must have clutched at his throat. Indeed, it would be unusual for a person in his predicament not to have experienced powerful anxiety that may even have bordered on panic.

Because our emotions play such a large part in our lives, we should consider how they operate. God created us emotional beings. His intent is that we respond to His love by loving and trusting Him.

### OUR FRAGILE EMOTIONS

It might surprise us to know that love is the only positive relational emotion. It is the opposite of fear (cf. I John 4:18). Ever since our first parents (Adam and Eve) sinned, we experience both love and fear. And because we possess a fallen, sinful nature, we are more accustomed to living with our fears than experiencing continuous affirmation and affection. In fact, we frequently fail to

---

[1] Thomas, *Genesis*, 128.

[2] As we have noted before, *fear* is present when we are confronted by a situation that has the power to deprive us of our freedom and also do us harm.

realize the prevalence of fear as an emotion because we have developed different ways of coping with it.

*Manifestations of Fear*

Fear manifests itself progressively in three different ways: First through anxiety, then through anger, and finally through guilt. Because we are human and prone to experience a sense of vulnerability, we become anxious about things—real or imagined—that lie outside the realm of our control. These upset us (e.g., a traffic jam, an illness, the faithlessness of a loved one, the truancy of one of our children, a court appearance, overdue bills, etc.). We fear that these things may curtail our freedom or prevent us from realizing some cherished plan. Of course, there are innumerable causes of anxiety. The antidote is trust in God's love for us. He is sovereign, and we should commit ourselves to living in conscious subjection to His will for us.

The Lord Jesus specifically stated that we are not to be overly anxious about the things of this life (cf. Matthew 6:25-34). By willingly remaining within His will, our anxieties can be reduced. And when we do feel fear rising in our hearts, we are instructed to lay our concerns at Christ's feet and have Him bear our burdens for us (I Peter 5:7).

When we do not succeed in coping with our anxieties or feelings of apprehension, we tend to become angry. Anger, we are told, is normally triggered by one or more of three things: *frustration* when our carefully laid plans miscarry or when we fail to measure up to our internalized ideals; *humiliation* when we feel we have failed or when

## Learning About People 163

someone has put us down and we have lost face with those about us; and *rejection* when we sense that we have been treated unjustly or thrust aside.

Hannah knew what it was like to feel frustrated. She had been unable to bear children and Peninah's ridicule of her was unrelenting. Hannah could have lashed out against her rival or clammed up, suppressing her true feelings. Instead, she took her problems to the Lord, and the quality of her relationship with Him was such that she could trust Him to answer her prayers (I Samuel 1).

David's ambassadors knew what humiliation was like. They had gone with a message of condolence to a neighboring king only to be treated shamefully. Half of their beards were shaved off and their long tunics were cut off at the hips. Obviously, they became the laughing stock of all who saw them, and they were forced to make their return journey to Judah with people from the towns and villages mocking them (II Samuel 20:4-5).

Samuel knew what it was like to be rejected (I Samuel 8). The elders of Israel came to him and demanded that he appoint a king to rule over them. Samuel could have reminded them of his lifetime of service or reprimanded them for their calloused ingratitude. Instead he took matters to the Lord in prayer. As he prayed he found that, while the people had rejected him, God had not. And because the Lord was more emotionally important to him than the people, his rejection by them was easier to bear. Furthermore, as he prayed, God gave him new confidence. He was led to accept what he could not change, and the Lord opened up new opportunities of service for him.

Anxiety (or apprehension) and anger are two of the non-relational emotions. The third is guilt. Guilt was experienced by Adam and Eve when they disobeyed God's express command and ate from a certain tree in the garden. Almost immediately, they became conscious of having violated His law, and so they hid from Him. Through their sin they lost their sense of security and set about developing plans for their wellbeing. They sewed fig leaves together.

But why did they find it necessary to try and hide from God? Is it possible that they did not realize their need for Him, and so did not seek reconciliation with God through confession and repentance? They sensed that they were vulnerable (i.e., insecure), and this must have been an acutely painful and bewildering experience for them.

Our efforts to maintain a sense of *security* have led us to develop and then refine certain coping mechanisms or "security operations." One of the first we read about in the Bible is *projection*—the attempt to rid ourselves of unacceptable behavior by blaming someone else. When God confronted Adam with his disobedience, Adam began by blaming both Eve and God; and Eve also used this strategy by blaming the serpent (Genesis 3:12-13).

Another defense mechanism that we encounter in the early chapters of Genesis is *displacement.* This technique of dealing with guilt involves the redirecting of an aggressive impulse toward a substitute person or object. Cain became angry because God accepted Abel's offering and did not accept the one he brought. Because God was too strong a person for him to vent his anger on, he took out his anger on his younger brother, Abel (Genesis 4:8). His hostile actions brought forth God's rebuke. Not being able to endure God's reproof, he withdrew and wandered about until he finally found a place to settle (Genesis 4:12-16).

A third method of coping with guilt is also easy to recognize. Throughout the centuries people have attempted to deal with the consequences of their guilt through *rationalization*. We have all resorted to this strategy when we have feared the loss of approval of either our elders or our peers. It is an attempt to excuse our behavior (and at the same time ease our feelings of guilt) by giving an acceptable "spin" to what we said or did. King Saul did this after he disobeyed the Lord. God told him to go and utterly destroy the Amalekites (I Samuel 15:1ff.). He and his men did attack the Amalekites, but they spared Agag and the best of the sheep and cattle. When Samuel confronted Saul with evidence of his disobedience, the king said, *"The people did it ... so that they could offer sacrifices to the Lord your God"* (I Samuel 15:13-16, noting v. 15). In other words, he rationalized his/their conduct (saying in effect, "Our motives were good; we did it so that we could honor the Lord").

Another strategy frequently resorted to when we desire to cover up failure in our churches or businesses is to appeal to *tradition*. This was the primary defense of the Pharisees. They determined how far a person could journey on the Sabbath without breaking the law (Acts 1:2), and which duties were binding and which were not (Mark 7:9-13). This was done in an attempt to assuage feelings of guilt. Those who do the same thing today invariably do so in order to excuse their failure before an authority figure. And if this authority figure is God, then (like the Pharisees) they want to appear in a favorable enough light to secure His favor (Mark 7:1-7, 20-23).

Another defensive mechanism—though the perpetrator is frequently unaware of it—is *compensation*. This involves responding to failure in one area by entering into another realm of activity where success is more likely. Jacob and Esau illustrate this tendency. Jacob could not compete with his brother in physical prowess like hunting and so compensated for his lack by becoming a gourmet chef. And Esau could not compete with Jacob's domestic skills and so excelled as an outdoorsman.

The "cousin" of compensation is *overcompensation.* This attempt to dodge the effects of guilt may be seen in exaggerated attempts to succeed (cf. Christ's indictment of the Pharisees in Matthew 23:14-31; Luke 11:42; 18:11-12). Lot may also have been guilty of overcompensation. He may have felt guilty about returning to live in Sodom (cf. II Peter 2:7-8), and so worked hard to become one of Sodom's leading citizens (even to becoming a judge, Genesis 19:1).

To try to minimize their sense of guilt, the Pharisees also practiced *reaction formation*—the repressing of socially unacceptable desires by taking on conscious attitudes and behavior that contradicted their true, unconscious wishes. Illustrations of this may be found throughout the gospels (e.g., Matthew 6:2-5).

Were the Pharisees kindly disposed toward people? Did they sustain good relationships with them? No. Their true attitude may be seen in their desire to apprehend the Lord Jesus and put Him to death (John 7:44-48: 11:47-53), even though they pretended before the people to be interested only in preserving the law. Furthermore, the Lord Jesus indicted them for greed that caused them to evict widows from their homes and deprive orphans of their inheritance.

A recounting of the subtle ways in which we try to deny our true feelings is not complete without mention of a trio of defensive strategies: *regression, repression,* and *suppression.*

Jonah regressed to an adolescent state of behavior when he chose to disobey God after being told to go to Nineveh and preach to the people living there. And Ahab did much the same when he was advised that he could not have Naboth's vineyard (I Kings 2:4).

David repressed from his conscious mind his sin with Bathsheba, and on account of this, experienced prolonged depression (Psalm 32:3-4).

And suppression—the hiding of one's true feelings out of fear that they will not be accepted—is illustrated in Amnon's desire for his half-sister, Tamar (II Samuel 13).

*Evidence of Love.* These negative emotional responses are very real. They govern much of our lives. Love, however, is the only positive relational emotion. True love is beautifully illustrated for us in the lives of Mary of Magdala[3] and the Apostle John.[4] And love—the seeking of the highest good in the one loved, even to the point of self-sacrifice—is the relational emotion that is to characterize the true disciple of Jesus Christ (cf. John 13:1; 15:13).

It is amazing how relevant and meaningful Bible study becomes when we understand how these emotions work in real life. Such an awareness causes well-known accounts and familiar Bible personalities to come alive. We also

---

[3] See C. J. Barber, *Vital Encounter* (1979), 123-32.

[4] *Ibid.,* 133-41.

find how much we have in common with those whom we read about on the pages of Scripture. We may summarize the emotional part of our beings as follows:

*Negative Relational Emotions*

Fear that manifests itself progressively through ...

A. **Anxiety** (Attributes two strengths to the object of one's anxiety or feeling of apprehension: *Almightiness* [the power to take away one's autonomy] and *impendency* [the power to do one harm]).

B. **Anger** (or Hostility) (Caused by feelings of *frustration, humiliation,* or *rejection*—and sometimes all three).

C. **Guilt** Improper Response: Defense mechanisms.

Proper Response: Confession leading to restoration.[5]

*Positive Relational Emotion: Love*

Desiring the highest good in the one loved even to the point of self-sacrifice.

---

[5] Other kinds of guilt—moral guilt, legal guilt, psychological guilt, and godly sorrow—have not been discussed here. A full discussion may be found in the author's commentary on II Samuel.

## UNHEEDED WARNING

As we have noted before, Lot, after having been delivered from Chedorlaomer by Abraham, again took up residence in Sodom. Any earlier feelings of *guilt* he may have had as he was led away ("God is punishing me for my forgetfulness of Him") and *apprehension* ("I wonder what will happen to me now?") may, after his rescue, have been replaced by the belief (rationalization): "God wasn't punishing me after all!" or the false confidence "Now that Chedorlaomer has been so thoroughly defeated, there is nothing to fear. No one else has the power to overthrow the armies of the kings of the valley."

In the course of time, however, *God* decided to destroy Sodom and Gomorrah (Genesis 18:20ff.; see also 19:24-25). He sent two angels (who appeared in the form of men) to Sodom to rescue Lot. Lot, we find, was sitting in the gate. He had become a judge. On seeing the men, he persuaded them to accept the hospitality of his home (Genesis 19:2). Their declining of Lot's offer may have been designed to test his sincerity. Lot, however, urged them strongly and they consented to be his houseguests for the night. And, as with Abraham, he prepared a feast for them (Genesis 19:3).

With nightfall, the men of the city thronged the streets outside Lot's home demanding that the visitors be turned over to them to satisfy their homosexual desires. Lot refused. His visitors had crossed the threshold of his home, and, according to ancient custom, it was his responsibility to protect them with his life (Genesis 19:8).[6]  As Dr. George Bush pointed out: "Lot insisted that the sacredness of the laws of hospitality protect them."[7]

How did Lot respond to the continued demands of the people of Sodom? He had spent his life achieving success through compromise. He had also had ample time to observe the perverted practices of the entrenched homosexuals who were now attempting to beat down his door. Realizing that in their advanced state of depravity they probably would not want sexual intercourse with women, he sought to placate them by offering them his daughters in place of the two strangers. This was not a loving act. How would he have felt if the men of Sodom had accepted his offer? Which defense mechanisms would he have used to try and ease his feelings of guilt?

## LIFE'S LABOR LOST

There is something else we need to notice in the story of Lot. In our last chapter, we outlined very briefly the hierarchy of needs. Lot attempted to find safety and sought it among the cities of the plain. He also wanted love and affection, and found it in a wife and family. He desired the esteem of his peers, and secured it by becoming one of Sodom's magistrates. All of this took time and effort. Now, however, in a single, decisive hour the scales of judgment are turned upside down. Instead of possessing

---

[6] H. C. Trumbull, *The Threshold Covenant* (1896), 335pp

[7] Bush, *Genesis*, I:305.

## Learning About People 171

influence and power in Sodom, the men of the city turned on him and scornfully threatened his life (Genesis 19:9). His sons-in-law, who were engaged[8] to his daughters, treated him with contempt (Genesis 19:14). And, when he finally fled Sodom, his wife was turned into a pillar of salt.[9] In the destruction of the city, he lost all that he had labored to accumulate (Genesis 19:24, 29).[10]

But Lot's troubles were not over. Only his daughters were left to him. They found shelter in a cave. His girls had been reared in Sodom and knew no motivation higher than the satisfaction of their basic needs. Fearing that they might never marry, each in turn made their father drunk and had sexual relations with him. Each conceived and bore a son (Genesis 19:30-38), and the names they gave their sons give no indication of either shame or remorse. While Lot believed them to be virgins at the time of the destruction of Sodom and Gomorrah, they were at heart strangers to virtue. And totally absent from anything they said or did was an awareness of the Lord God, or of their accountability to Him.

What were Lot's thoughts as he looked out over the Dead Sea basin the next morning and saw the smoldering ruins of the place that had at one time been his home? We

---

[8] "Engagement" in Bible times was a serious affair. The couple was looked upon as married even though they had not begun to live together and had not yet had sexual intercourse.

[9] H. Rimmer, *Lot's Wife and the Science of Physics* (1947), 160pp.

[10] Davis, *Paradise to Prison*, 203.

do not know. Sufficient to say that, apart from his flocks and herds that were outside the city, he had lost everything.

Are riches therefore wrong?

No, they are not. Consider Abraham; he was rich. The difference between Abraham and Lot was that Abraham wasn't interested in riches, whereas Lot was. The focal point of Abraham's life was walking in fellowship with the Lord (Hebrews 11:8ff.). The center of Lot's life was himself. Abraham was not without his imperfections, but his life demonstrated continuous spiritual growth. Lot was in all probability a most capable and likeable person, but the choices he made led him away from the Lord, and in the end he lost everything that was dear to him.

Because there is something of Lot in all of us, this summary by Dr. W. H. Griffith Thomas is most apropos:

- The first danger Lot faced was from things lawful. It was not wrong to desire a good place for his flocks and herds. His sin was in putting earthly ease and prosperity first.

- Another danger was compromise. At first Lot pitched his tent *toward* Sodom, but soon he entered the city and stayed there.

- A third danger that Lot incurred was that of worldliness. He showed genuine hospitality, but his character was weakened, and his life was essentially selfish from the moment that he chose the best part of the land to the moment when he was prepared to sacrifice his daughters....

- Lot lacked the spirit of true independence. He was all right as long as he was with the stronger Abraham....
- He also lacked decision. At every point of the story, we observe his indecision. It appears stamped on his character (Genesis 19:16, 17*b*-21, 30).[11]

## INTERACTION

Imagine you are in Sodom amid the events that are described in Genesis 19. If you are meeting with a group, divide into three sections so that each section can work with one of the following passages of Scripture: Genesis 19:1-11, 19:12-22; and 30-38. Make a list of the possible emotional responses of Lot, his visitors, the men of Sodom, Lot's sons-in-law, his wife, and his daughters. Discuss these emotions within your group, and then share your findings with the others. If you are studying on your own, tackle the same assignment one section at a time. Then, if possible, share your insights with a friend.

---

[11] Thomas, *Genesis*, 128-29.

Chapter Twelve

# THE CONNECTION BETWEEN BEING AND DOING

## THE ETHICAL METHOD

Two young boys were sitting in church. The one boy's father was the pastor. When his dad got up to preach, he began his topic by giving a dictionary definition of the biblical word he was about to expound. His son leaned over, nudged his friend, and said in a loud whisper, "Preachers always do that when they don't know what else to say."

We cannot dispute the young lad's observation, but his statement is not a truism. Sometimes a definition clarifies the parameters of a topic. The *Random House Dictionary of the English Language* defines "ethics" as follows:

1. The body of moral principles or values governing or distinctive of a particular culture.

2. A complex of moral precepts held or rules of conduct ....[1]

---

[1] *Random House Dictionary of the English Language*, ed. J. Stein (1969), 489.

The definition is clear, but with three out of four people in the United States claiming that there is no such thing as absolute truth, how can any group settle on a distinctive set of values or moral precepts? The argument is advanced that no two people will see things quite alike, so how can one person impose his or her values on another? But the question remains, How then can a society establish a set of norms to guide its behavior? And without definable values, how can we or our children know what is best?

We conclude from this impasse that there needs to be an external, objective standard by which people can govern their lives. Judaism, for example, has the Ten Commandments, and these rules have regulated and safeguarded them for millennia. In time, Christianity inherited the Old Testament and saw the wisdom of this ancient Decalogue. But such time-honored principles have recently been banned in our schools and courtrooms. In place of any definable values, we have been compelled to follow the lead of those who would legislate "political correctness," while tacitly denying the importance of spiritual and moral correctness.

And so we have permeating throughout our society, and condoned by officials in high places, the practice of lying under oath, deliberate acts of deceit, immoral behavior, graft, and the willful distortion of our Constitution by those who have sworn to uphold it.

Accompanying the decline in ethical standards is an insidious "blame game." Whenever something goes wrong the cry goes up, "Who is to blame?" In many instances, this takes the form of "scapegoating." A person or organization is sought and the blame for a particular failure is

## The Connection Between Being and Doing 177

fixed on the individual or group. In the process, reputations or careers are ruined. It is no wonder, therefore, that the "Golden Rule," *"And as you would that men should do to you, do likewise to them"* (Luke 6:31), has been rewritten to read "Do it to others before they do it to you."

In light of this moral interregnum, we have to face our own hypocrisy. As more and more discussion takes place on the meaning and purpose of life (while exposing the horrors of genocide, the plight of "runaway" kids, threat of violence in our schools, gangs, senseless shooting in residential areas, "highway rage," etc), we are confronted by the fact that our legal system appears powerless to stop these violations of human rights and the diminution of human dignity. Little change, therefore, can be expected. And the reason? The beliefs and values that have been the mainstay of our American culture in the past have been set aside. People of integrity are frequently denied advancement and derided for their standard of ethics.[2] Intimidators are the ones who most often get ahead, while others are labeled "puritan" or "unbending" or "out of step with the times."

To make matters worse, we have stood aside as our history has been rewritten, and we have not protested when the mainstream media daily biases the minds of citizens so that aberrations in thought and action have become

---

[2] Witness, for example, the Los Angeles Police Department. When Daryl Gates was forced out of office, Bob Vernon was in line for the position of Police Chief. He was denied promotion because of his beliefs, and the local media caricatured him as a *fundamentalist* Christian (with emphasis on "fundamentalist"). The result? Los Angeles has had a series of police chiefs and a record of scandals that has tarnished the record of the city.

normative. Furthermore, as we have watched the evening news on TV we have seen reporters use a mantra of cliches (e.g., reverence for the family, an emphasis on education, pursuing the "American dream," etc.) to mask the way in which they have downgraded righteousness, while heralding sin (in its various forms) as an expression of personal freedom.

Our institutions of higher learning pretend to be interested in the problems facing us as a nation, but they lack the will to expose the fundamental difference between good and evil, right and wrong, and so focus only on obvious violations of human rights (e.g., the Holocaust, racism, women's rights, etc.). The courses in ethics taught in these places of higher learning invariably concentrate on the history of ethics (e.g., Chinese, Babylonian, Greek), or sociological matters (e.g., slums, teenage pregnancies), or the viewpoints of a particular individual (e.g., Kant, Hegel, Descartes, Rousseau, Mill). As insightful as these approaches may be, they leave many questions unanswered. And because they also lack an *inherent objective authority*, people are left to choose or to reject what they have been taught.

In light of the confusion that is evident on every hand, Christians may validly ask, "What are we to do? Is there an answer to this dilemma?"

Joseph Fletcher, in his book, *Situation Ethics*, outlined a system of conduct based on a "contextual ethic." He positioned different schools of thought on a horizontal line. Norman L. Geisler, in *Ethics: Alternitives and Issues*

---

[3] J. F. Fletcher, *Situation Ethics* (1966), 176pp.

deftly analyzed the theories and varying theorists on a vertical continuum. He then sought to establish criteria whereby a person should "choose the highest good."[4] But these systems leave readers confused over which approach to adopt. In light of the perplexing (and often contradictory) theories discussed, it is no wonder that the average person has become frustrated and disillusioned. And so we are left to ask ourselves, "Is there an answer that is simple enough for us to grasp and workable enough to guide us through the enigmatic situations we face in the course of our lives?"

The answer is, "Yes." It may surprise us to know that in Genesis, chapter 20, we have an important *clue* regarding true ethics and a life of freedom. It will prove helpful for you to read over the chapter and jot down in your notebook each reference or allusion to principles of right conduct. Once this has been done, you will be able to go back over the chapter and take note of the phrase, *"the fear of God"* (Genesis 20:11). Then, as you look back to verse 6, you will note the fact that sin, whether intentional or unintentional, is regarded as being committed against God. This is an important point to remember. People who excuse their behavior by saying, "But everybody's doing it," or "What harm can it do provided no one gets hurt?" show by their attitude that they do not believe they are accountable to God. But they are. His standards, therefore, are important to each one of us.

The Old Testament as well as the New has a great deal to say about the *"fear of the Lord."*

---

[4] N. L. Geisler, *Ethics: Alternatives and Issues* (1971), 270pp.

The kind of fear we have all experienced falls into two primary categories, the one beneficial and the other harmful. In the former, fear of danger leads us to take wise precautions to insure our safety and to protect the ones we love. This is healthy. In the latter case, however, fear may arise over something insignificant, and, because we do not handle it appropriately, it becomes a source of anxiety that may be mild or severe depending on the cause. This is unhealthy. The Lord Jesus, while on earth, counseled people on how to handle their fears. He said in effect, "Do not become overly anxious about the things of this life—what you shall eat, or what you shall drink. Instead of worrying about these things, consider the birds ... and trust God to take care of you" (see Matthew 6:25-32).

The *"fear of the Lord"* differs from these kinds of fear, although it is related to them. It may best be described as living in reverential awe of God, and is comprised of two fundamental elements: repulsion and attraction. On the one hand is apprehension of God that elicits dread, the fear of punishment, and on the other hand, there is an attraction that draws us to the Lord who loves us.

Scripture introduces us to the former when we read of Adam after he sinned. When God came looking for him, Adam said: *"I heard the sound of You in the garden, and I was afraid because I was naked; so I hid myself"* (Genesis 3:10. See also Deuteronomy 17:13; 21:21; Matthew 10:28; Hebrews 4:1; 10:27, 31—where dread of judgment is in view). Fear of just retribution led Adam to withdraw. God is holy. We are responsible to Him. Sin is a violation of His nature. We fear His wrath and so flee from Him.

The fear of the Lord also involves attraction. It acknowledges God's power and might, recognizes His

# The Connection Between Being and Doing

authority, and as a creature before the Creator, it acknowledges that there is no meaningful existence apart from Him. And so we come to Him in repentance asking for His forgiveness.

There is in this reverential awe of God an all-pervasive sense of His presence (Psalm 139:7-10). Everything we do is under His watchful eye. This is coupled with a deeply ingrained awareness of our dependence on Him (Psalm 139:1-6. 13-16, 23-24; Acts 17:26-28; Romans 11:36; I Corinthians 8:6; Hebrews 2:10; Revelation 4:11), for as creatures it is incumbent upon us to do His will.

But how can we know His will?

We can only know the will of God through a constant, conscious, personal relationship with Him. And this vertical God-consciousness is essential if our lives are to be lived in a way that pleases Him.

### *Diametrically Opposed*

A few biblical examples will help us understand what we have been describing. First, let us think of Job. When Satan appeared before the Lord, God inquired, *"Have you considered My servant Job?* ***For there is no one like him on the earth, a blameless and upright man, fearing God and turning away from evil***" (Job 1:8; 2:3, emphasis added). Job's integrity was vitally related to his *"fearing"* God (i.e., living in reverential awe of Him).

Isaiah also serves as an illustration of one overawed by the holiness of God. He had a vision of God seated on His throne, and this brought his true condition into focus. He knew himself to be sinful. His response was immediate:

> *"Woe is me, for I am ruined!*
> *Because I am a man of unclean lips,*
> *And I live among a people of unclean lips;*
> *For my eyes have seen the King, the LORD of hosts"* (Isaiah 6:5).

Reverence for God is the basis of ethics. It brings the fundamental issues of life into perspective. It is also the foundation of our willing service. In Isaiah's case, the Lord cleansed his sin and commissioned him to bear a message to His people.

When Abraham did not see the *"fear of God"* in the eyes of the people of Gerar, he became anxious (Genesis 20:11; cf. Proverbs 8:13). He knew that ethical standards regulate respect for human life and institutions (such as marriage), and without them, he feared dealing with the people.

### *Changing Attitudes*

We come to a clearer understanding of the *"fear of the Lord"* when we check a concordance under "fear." We can then select all the references that deal specifically with *"fear of the Lord"* or *"fear of God."* We find the essence of this teaching to involve keeping God's commandments (Exodus 20:20), obeying His word (Deuteronomy 6:13, 24; Psalm 5:7), taking time to listen to what He has to say to us, and doing His will (I Samuel 12:14).

Walking in obedience to the Lord gives us confidence (Psalm 33:18-19), and this is said to prolong life while also investing it with joy (Proverbs 10:27; 14:27; 22:4. Cf. Psalm 61:5; 119:37ff.). It's that simple!

## The Supreme Example

As we continue our study of the *"fear of the Lord,"* we come across something surprising. Isaiah predicted that the Messiah, the Lord Jesus Christ, would live in the fear of the Lord. His words are well-known: *"The Spirit of the LORD will rest on Him, the spirit of wisdom and understanding, the spirit of counsel and strength, the spirit of knowledge and **the fear of the LORD.** **And He will delight in the fear of the LORD**, and He will not judge by what His eyes see, nor make a decision by what His ears hear; but with righteousness He will judge the poor, and decide with fairness for the afflicted of the earth; and He will strike the earth with the rod of His mouth, and with the breath of His lips He will slay the wicked. Also righteousness will be the belt about His loins, and faithfulness the belt about His waist"* (Isaiah 11:2-5, emphasis added).

As we read these verses, it is interesting to note the close link between the fear of the Lord and right conduct (or proper ethics). It is no wonder, therefore, that the writer of Hebrews applied the Messianic prophecy of Psalm 40:7-8 to the Lord Jesus (Hebrews 10:7; cf. John 4:34; 6:38). And rightly did Peter say of Him that He left us an example that we should follow in His steps (I Peter 2:21).

How did the Lord Jesus achieve all that He set out to do? By walking in the fear of the Lord!

## Our Social Masks

The Word of God is filled with practical examples of people who were kept from evil, actual or potential, because they walked in the fear of the Lord.

- The fear of sinning against God kept Joseph from committing adultery with Potiphar's wife (Genesis 39:4-15), in spite of the fact that she tried daily to seduce him.

- The dread of God's judgments led to the repentance of Rahab, the harlot of Jericho (Joshua 2:9. Cf. Joshua 10:2, 10).

- Nehemiah, when he became governor of the impoverished province of Judah, did not take the legitimate salary out of reverential awe of God (Nehemiah 5:6-15).

In summary, the Old Testament use of the *"fear of the Lord"* states that it should give us compassion for the disabled (Leviticus 19:14) as well as respect for the aged (Leviticus 19:32); provide us with principles for governing our interpersonal relationships (Leviticus 25:17; Deuteronomy 6:10-15; 10:12); become the basis for a sound administration/system of government (Leviticus 25:43; Deuteronomy 17:19; I Kings 8:40-43); be the first fundamental of prayer (Nehemiah 1:11); enable us to witness successfully (Deuteronomy 5:29; 6:24); provide us with guidance in child-rearing (Deuteronomy 6:1-2, 20-25); lay a foundation for acceptable service (Deuteronomy 10:20; I Samuel 12:24); be the prerequisite for acceptable stewardship (Deuteronomy 14:23); and serve as a rebuke of formalism (Isaiah 29:13).

By walking in the fear of the Lord, King Asa was given the victory over his enemies (II Chronicles 14:14), King Jehoshaphat enjoyed God's protection (II Chronicles 17:10; 20:29), and the psalmist affirmed that the fear of the

Lord left no place for the fear of other people (Psalm 118:6).

## *Liberty Versus Legalism and License*

Different ethical systems have exaggerated either the wrath or the love of God. The errors that have grown up around these teachings have a direct bearing on one's happiness, sense of well-being, and ability to respond to God's grace. Legalism versus license may best be described by a continuum with legalism at the one end and license at the other.

An exaggerated emphasis on God's punishment leads to legalism (i.e., a set of rules or a moral code that becomes an inflexible standard by which the practitioner believes that he or she can avoid incurring God's displeasure). A biblical illustration of this would be Pharisaism. Legalism occurs whenever we have man-made rules taking the place of the Word of God. This same kind of situation lies at the root of pagan religions where an individual sets up a false deity or deities and insists on some form of ritual worship.

The same distortions (though at the other end of the continuum) are true in situations where there is an overemphasis on the love of God. Those who stress His "love" and ignore His other attributes make a "god" for themselves who will condone their evil practices and not punish them for their sins (Romans 1:18-32). This leads to license, and the sensual worship of many pagan religions illustrates this very clearly.

C. S. Lewis observed that some Christians are so afraid of being identified with those who are laissez-faire (i.e., licentious) in their lifestyle that they inadvertently back into a legalistic position. Which brings to the fore the question, "How then can a Christian enjoy the liberty of which the Bible speaks?"

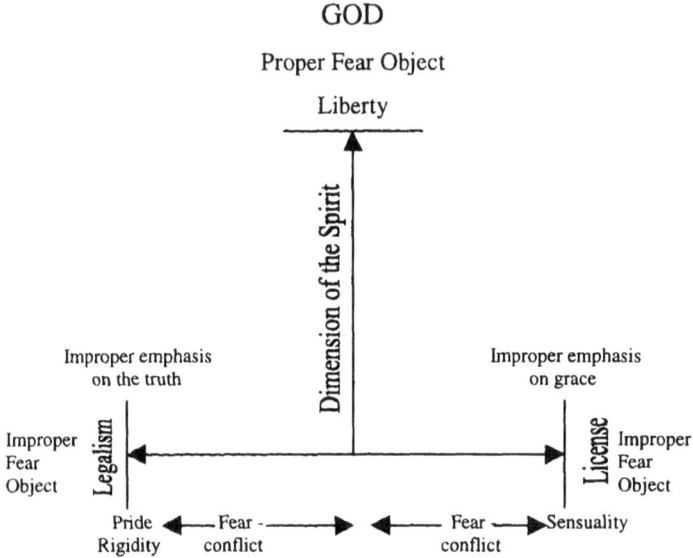

Both systems—legalism and license—are found in modern movements where stress is placed on a creed or set of rules, or else favor a belief system that redefines principles of right and wrong leaving people free to choose their own "good." Such extremes ignore the fact that God has set the standard (I Corinthians 7:1; I Peter 1:15-16). The essence of His standard is His holiness, and this involves separation—separation *from* the world's system of values *to* God's standards and values (Deuteronomy 6:4-19). The worldly elite of Nehemiah's day could exploit people of their own race because they did not live in reverential awe of God. Nehemiah, however, exercised godly compassion. He could say, "I did not do so because of the fear of my God" (Nehemiah 5:15). Real reverence for God leads to uprightness of life (Proverbs 8:13). It brings us to a place in our experience where we gladly do His will (Ecclesiastes 12:13). And it places us in a position whereby we can enjoy the blessings of His love (Deuteronomy 5:29; Psalm 147:11). He becomes the Object of our reverence (i.e., our proper fear-Object). By living in the Spirit we avoid the opposing tensions of the flesh (Romans 8:2).

In reality, legalism and license are improper fear-objects. When we operate on the level of the flesh, we gravitate either toward the indulgence of our desires (through the fear that life may pass us by and we will not have enjoyed all it has to offer) or else we back away from known sin (for fear of retribution). This generates a fear-conflict. Only as we hold God in the supreme position as Lord do we enjoy perfect liberty.[5] And it is only as we walk in reverential awe of God that we can *"love God with all our heart, and love our neighbor as ourselves"* (cf. Mark 12:30-31).

## INTERACTION

1. Discuss Abraham's conduct in Gerar in light of the fear of the Lord. Where did he go wrong? Why? What should he have done? Who got hurt? What may we learn from his experience?

---

[5] Barber, *Nehemiah*, 71, 99-108.

2. Abimelech and his people were more righteous than Abraham. What does this teach us about (a) our fears, and (b) judging by appearances?

3. By working with your Bible concordance, construct a table of the teaching of the New Testament on the fear of the Lord. What does this teach us about specific principles of right and wrong, as well as our attitudes and conduct?

Chapter Thirteen

# THE GOAL OF LIFE

## THE DEVOTIONAL METHOD

The goal of every Christian should be conformity to the image of Christ. But how is this attained? Simply put, it is becoming rooted and grounded in the Word of God. Paul wrote: *"Therefore as you have received Christ Jesus the Lord, so walk in Him, having been firmly rooted and now being built up in Him and established in your faith, just as you were instructed, and overflowing with gratitude"* (Colossians 2:6-7).

Mark Hatfield, former senator from Oregon, wrote:

> I do not regard the Bible as a bedtime story to prepare me for a restful night, nor is it simply an order of worship to be used on Sunday mornings. Since it is the source of God's truth, we need to be saturated with it. We need to delve into it systematically, with enthusiasm, with curiosity, and with a willingness to apply God's will as it unfolds to us.[1]

---

[1] *Christianity Today* (November 22, 1963), 4.

When Professor Martin J. Buerger, director of advanced studies in the Massachusetts Institute of Technology, and a world-renowned scientist, was questioned about his use of the Bible, he said:

> If one regards [the Bible] as the Scripture inspired by God, it becomes not just another piece of literature but a unique piece of literature worthy of more than casual attention. ... I find the Bible worth reading again and again to remind me of many things I already know, but that are forced into the back of my mind by the daily traffic of new impressions.[2]

It is important that our study of God's Word be personal. Dr. Merrill C. Tenney, whose book, *Galatians: Charter of Christian Liberty*, deserves to be read and reread, stated:

> Devotional study is not so much a technique as a spirit. It is the spirit of eagerness which seeks the mind of God; it is the spirit of humility which listens readily to the voice of God; it is the spirit of adventure which pursues earnestly the will of God; it is the spirit of adoration which rests in the presence of God.[3]

But spiritual growth and the blessings that accompany a God-centered life are not automatic. It takes time for us to grow to maturity. And this involves obedience from the

---

[2] *Ibid*, 4.

[3] Tenney, *Galatians*, 207-08.

heart to the things that are taught in the Bible. Only then does God bestow upon us His special blessings.

## *Of Risks and Rewards*

We need to remember that the devotional method of Bible study grows out of the application of Scripture to life. It is dynamic and effects changes in our attitudes, beliefs, and values. It utilizes the skills of observation and interpretation. It also utilizes other methods of investigation—historical, cultural, social, doctrinal, biographical—but differs from them in that the aim of this method is to worship God in spirit and in truth (John 4:24). Its goal is the glory of God (Ephesians 1:5-6,12,14). In the process we are able to sharpen our powers of discernment (Hebrews 5:13-14). This was the psalmist's experience (Psalm 119:97-104).

The Bible contains some important specifics regarding the time, nature, content, and purpose of our study of God's Word (cf. Joshua 1:8). Experience confirms the need for our regular exposure to our heavenly Father's teaching. This requires discipline. Then, we should have a regular place where distractions are minimal. We should also approach this time of study in the proper attitude (Isaiah 30:15c; Psalm 46:1ff.; 95:6). And finally, we should show by our conduct that our lives are Christ-centered (as opposed to being self-centered), and that we live under the authority of God's Word. This will pave the way for true worship.

### Unpromising Situation

In order to learn more about this intensely personal method of Bible study, let us look at an intensely personal event in the life of Abraham (Genesis 22). The story is easily told, but it is not as easily understood, for God instructed Abraham to go to Mount Moriah and offer up his son Isaac as a burnt offering.

Our initial reaction is to become so preoccupied with God's command in verse 2 that we fail to look for the main teaching of the passage. "How can God be righteous and command such a thing?" we ask. And, because we abhor human sacrifices, we cannot see how this passage could have any relevance for us, let alone be for our edification.

In light of our cultural difficulties, we should look at God's command first to find out what His purpose was in instructing Abraham to sacrifice his son. The renowned Semitic scholar of Grace Theological Seminary, Dr. John Davis, summarized the different approaches for us:

> A large group of scholars contend that human sacrifice was a custom in Abraham's day, and this passage must be seen in that context. Advocates of this position usually adopt a more or less revolutionary approach to Israel's religion. Human sacrifice was unquestionably practiced in Old Testament times. A Babylonian cylinder seal, for example, unmistakably portrays the execution of a human sacrifice, and the translation of an Akkadian poem describes the sacrifice of a first-born son.... The best approach to the passage is that God commanded an actual sacrifice and

Abraham intended to obey him fully. Such a conclusion may seem harsh, but it is in keeping with the language of the text and in harmony with the outcome. God later prohibited human sacrifice in the Mosaic Law, and while He commanded Abraham to perform it, He then prevented Him from practicing it. This largely relieves the moral tension. The only sacrifice of a human which God has required and accepted was that of His own Son, who was a propitiation for our sins. And it should be remembered that Jesus Christ was no mere man; as the God-Man He provided a substitutionary atonement which is eternal.[4]

Further difficulty in interpreting this passage is removed when we realize that God set out to "try" or "prove" Abraham (Genesis 22:1; cf. James 1:12-15)—as He often does us. In Abraham's case, this was done not for the purpose of God gaining information about His servant, but in order to manifest to us and to others the prevailing disposition of Abraham's heart.[5] (And, of course, when He tests us, it is to show us the disposition of our own hearts.)

To understand the significance of the test, we need to note the words with which this chapter begins: *"After these things."* They immediately refer us back to the preceding chapter. Several years had passed since Abraham settled near Gerar. Isaac was born and grew to young manhood. And Abraham had continued to become more and more

---

[4] Davis, *Paradise to Prison*, 216-18.

[5] Bush, *Genesis*, II:4.

influential in the area. It was in recognition of his greatness that Abimelech (the king of a city-state) and Phicol (commander of Abimelech's army) came to Abraham and expressed their desire to enter into a treaty with him (Genesis 21:22-34). They recognized that he had become a great and powerful man.

It was after the respect and honor paid the patriarch by Abimelech, that the Lord tested him. And it is the same in our experience. After the blessing of the summer camp, for example, there is the return home where people know our weaknesses and failings and can predict our attitudes and actions. And after the spiritual enrichment of the message last Lord's day there comes Monday morning and a return to our places of business.

Now put yourself in Abraham's position. How would you feel, after this high point in your experience, if God appeared to you and told you to go and offer as a sacrifice that which was dearer to you than life itself?

In this connection, Abraham's trial was not unlike the testing that we face at different times during our Christian lives. God tests us with the things we hold closest to our hearts. This point was illustrated for me several years ago. Phil, one of my students, was dating a fine young girl named Peggy. Their romance blossomed and matured and I expected that an announcement of their engagement would be forthcoming. One day after lunch, I received an unexpected visit from Peggy. She was very upset.

"What's the matter?" I asked.

Peggy fought bravely to stem the flow of her tears. Finally she managed to sob out the story.

"Phil and I have broken up."

# The Goal of Life 195

"Why?" I asked. "What has brought about this crisis in your relationship?"

"Phil wants to be a missionary," Peggy sobbed, "and he doesn't think I will make a good missionary wife."

I comforted Peggy as best I could, and promised to talk to Phil.

When I discussed with Phil the events that led to the breaking off his relationship with Peggy, he had a slightly different story, but the main points were the same.

"How do you feel about Peggy?" I asked.

"I still love her. I'm not giving her up for someone else. I probably will never meet anyone as fine as Peggy the rest of my life."

"Then why are you breaking up with her?"

"I was born on the mission field. I know what it is like. I don't believe a person has the right to expect a wife to follow him to the mission field and share that kind of life!" he stated emphatically.

"It is very noble of you to feel that way, Phil," I countered, "but don't you think that is a decision Peggy should make?"

Phil was silent for a while. I observed him closely. Tears formed in his eyes, and one that refused to be controlled rolled down his cheek. He brushed it aside and breathed deeply.

"Phil," I said, breaking the silence, "I don't think your situation is unique. In fact, I find that something similar happened in the life of Abraham. God tested him to see where his priorities lay. He told him to take Isaac and offer him as a sacrifice on Mount Moriah. Abraham met the challenge and, in doing so, showed God that He came first in his life. In much the same way, you have done as Abraham did. You have shown that you are prepared to give up the best relationship you could ever have for a life of sacrificial service. Before taking matters further, why not consider before the Lord whether this incident from the life of Abraham has any application to your situation, and whether God might be saying to you, in effect, 'Don't take matters any further. Now I know that you reverence Me, since you have not withheld from Me that which was most precious to you.'"

A year later I conducted the wedding ceremony for Phil and Peggy, and shortly thereafter they left for language school in South America. They are still on the mission field and continue to work together effectively as a couple.

God often tests our relationship to love-objects—people, personal desires, possessions—to show us where our affections really lie. He does this not because He needs to know where we stand, but with a view to testing us so that we may be brought to greater maturity as a result of the process.

## *Prompt Obedience*

As we continue our devotional study of Genesis 22, consider Abraham's response in verses 3 and 4.[6] It was

---

[6] God may have spoken to Abraham in a dream or vision during the night, for "he arose early" to do as the Lord had instructed him. Such appearances of "the God of glory" (Acts 7:2) are different from the claims of cultists who claim to hear voices or who conduct bizarre rituals in the name of God.

prompt. He never questioned what God said to him. By his actions, he demonstrated that he lived under the authority of God's revealed will. This point is important: No reluctance, no hesitation, no doubt marked his conduct (cf. Psalm 119:59-60).

What do you think he told Sarah? Possibly much the same as he told the men who accompanied him and Isaac to Mount Moriah: "We're going to offer a sacrifice to the Lord, and when we've done so, we will return to you."

Next, notice that it took Abraham and his little party *"three days"* to reach their destination. There was plenty of time for a vacillating heart to concoct some sort of compromise. But Abraham did not look for a way out. His heart was fixed on doing what God wanted done.

It seems evident from verse 5 that Abraham's theology sustained him. God's recent instructions seemed totally out-of-keeping with His earlier promise. God had said, *"You shall have a son"* and, *"In Isaac shall your seed be called"* (Genesis 17:19,21; 21:12; cf. Romans 9:7; Hebrews 11:17-19). If Isaac were slain, how could God's promises be fulfilled?

Abraham believed that from the ashes of the burnt offering[7] God could raise his son to life again. And with the confidence which faith inspires, Abraham said to his young men, *"Stay here with the donkey, and I and the lad will go yonder; and we will worship and return to you"* (Genesis 22:5).

---

[7] A burnt offering is one that is wholly consumed. No part of it is withheld.

The simplicity of Abraham's faith is remarkable. It was the result of his many years of walking with the Lord. His confidence in God was implicit. His reliance on the Lord was complete. In such a response, Abraham continued to enjoy the rest of faith.

## Timely Intervention

The sequence of events in verses 9-12 needs little comment. Isaac's attitude is most impressive. He was a lad in his mid- to late teens and could easily have resisted his father. He, however, must have shared his father's belief that, if sacrificed, he would rise again from the ashes of the burnt offering.

After Isaac was bound and lay on the altar, the Lord intervened in a most dramatic way. At the precise moment that Abraham was about to carry out God's command, the Angel of the Lord called to him: *"Abraham, Abraham! ... Do not stretch out your hand against the lad, and do nothing to him; for now I know that you fear [reverence] God, since you have not withheld your son, your only son, from Me"* (Genesis 22:11-12).

Glancing around, Abraham found a ram caught in the bushes, and he offered it to the Lord as a burnt offering in place of Isaac. Through this experience, Abraham's understanding of God and His ways was enlarged. In recognition of the new understanding he received, he called the place Jehovah-jireh, *"the Lord will provide."*[8]

---

[8] The events of this chapter cast a "shadow" down the centuries and prefigure other events. For example, Isaac illustrates the obedience of Christ (Philippians 2:5-8); Abraham prefigures the actions

# The Goal of Life

Centuries later, on that same mountain (II Chronicles 3:1), Solomon built the Temple; and on that same ridge (now severed from the crest of the hill by a road), the cross bearing the Lord Jesus was dropped into a socket hollowed out of the rock. God did provide a suitable sacrifice to atone for the sin of mankind.

It was after Abraham's faith had been tested that the Lord spoke to him a second time (Genesis 22:15-18). He reaffirmed His covenant with him and specifically stated that it would be through Isaac, his *"seed"* (singular), that all the nations of the world would be blessed (Galatians 3:8, 16).

God is very precise. He has included information in His Word for us to uncover which, when we do so, reveals to us the amazing consistency and reliability of all that is taught in the Bible.[9]

---

of God the Father who did not spare His own Son, but freely offered Him up for us all (John 3:16; Romans 8:32); the ram pictures for us the substitutionary death of Christ (Hebrews 10:5-10); and Isaac's rising up from off the altar typifies the resurrection (Hebrews 11:19). The teaching of the passage is reinforced by James, our Lord's brother (see James 2:21-22) in which Abraham's obedience is evidence of his faith in God.

[9] Ryrie has an interesting note on Galatians 3:16 in *The Ryrie Study Bible* (p.1869). He points out that the Apostle Paul must have believed in the accuracy of the very words of Scripture to base his argument on the singular form of the word "seed."

## *It's the Relationship That Counts*

Our experience of different trials is unlikely to be as dramatic as Abraham's. God, however, does test us, and it is only after we have obeyed His will that He blesses us.

We may not always receive an explanation for the trials we are called upon to endure; but whether the trial is of short duration or lasts a lifetime, God is at work in us. He uses His Word to encourage our hearts when the vicissitudes of life seem overwhelming, and He uses the processes through which we pass to bring us to greater maturity.

Our fellowship with the Lord, therefore, should gradually transform[10] us into the image of Christ (II Corinthians 3:18).

## *Looking Back*

As we consider Genesis 22 and its application to our lives, let us remember three important principles:

- We should expect times of testing.
- We should live in obedience to the revealed will of God.
- We should wait patiently for the Lord to accomplish His work in us.

---

[10] Christ, in Mark 4:28 likened our spiritual growth to the growth of grain. Its progress can be measured.

Abraham did. He found that obedience is the key to blessing.

### INTERACTION

1. In reviewing the material we have covered in this chapter, put yourself in the position of Isaac. What might his thoughts have been en route to Mount Moriah? What is indicated in the text? Does his willing acquiescence to be bound and placed on the altar indicate trust in his father, or God, or both? How might his voluntary submission (for he was a lad between 15 and 17 at the time, and strong enough to resist his father, Abraham) parallel your experience with your heavenly Father?

2. The study of biblical symbolism (typology) has been described as: "An action or occurrence in which one event, person, or circumstance is intended to represent another, similar to it in certain respects, but of more importance, and generally future" (see Colossians 2:17; Hebrews 10:1).[11] It has also been described as emblematic or symbolic, and as such is used to express, embody, represent, or forecast some person, truth, or event. It is one of the most eloquent forms of figurative teaching in Scripture.[12] (See footnote #8.) In what way, therefore, does the ram offered

---

[11] B. Nichols, *Helps in Bible Reading* (1847), 147.

[12] A. T. Pierson, *The Bible and Spiritual Criticism* (1970), 184.

in the place of Isaac illustrate or prefigure the substitutionary sacrifice of Christ? Imagine again that you are Isaac. How important would the ram's death be to you? Enumerate your thoughts.

3. In Genesis 22:16-18, God renews the Abrahamic Covenant. How do you think Abraham felt when he returned to his camp? What was the effect of the confirmation of this covenant on him? Can we expect some similar reaffirmation of God's blessing of us?

Chapter Fourteen

# REAPING THE REWARDS

## THE TOPICAL METHOD

You are about to enter one of the most fruitful and rewarding areas of Bible study. It is also one of the most challenging. It is easy to study topics like "father" or "son," "husband" or "wife," "heart" and "soul," or the fruit of the Spirit, *viz.*, "love, joy, peace, patience, kindness, goodness, faithfulness, gentleness, and self-control." These are the usual topics of interest, and after each word has been studied with the aid of your concordance and Bible dictionary, further information can be gleaned from a book like *Vine's Complete Expository Dictionary of Old and New Testament Words* (1985), by M. F. Unger, W. White, Jr., and W. E. Vine.

Also of special interest, and of a more challenging nature, is the research of topics like *the "hem of the garment"* motif (Matthew 9:20; 14:36), the significance of *"thirty pieces of silver"* (Exodus 21:32; Leviticus 27:4; Matthew 26:15), why Shechem was called *the "navel of the earth"* (Genesis 12:6; etc.), exactly what was Leviathan? (Job 3:8; 41:1; Psalm 104:26; Isaiah 27:1), the significance of *"milk and honey"* (Exodus 3:8; Deuteronomy 27:3; cf. Psalm 81:16), and what we are to understand *by "windows in heaven"* (Genesis 7:11; 2 Kings 7:2; Malachi 3:10).

But this is not all. The topical or thematic method of Bible study, rightly understood and rightly applied, can be enormously satisfying. It builds upon the other methods of investigation and involves (1) studying a special subject or theme throughout the entire Bible or a book of the Bible; or (2) studying a passage of Scripture which highlights a specific topic (e.g., service, stewardship, faithfulness).

An example of the former of these methods is illustrated for us by Merrill C. Tenney in *Galatians: Charter of Christian Liberty.* In his book, Dr. Tenney uses the word *nomos*, "law," and traces its use by Paul in the letter to the Galatians. Other word studies (e.g., marriage, fellowship, truth/truthfulness) can also be undertaken, depending on the frequency of their use by a particular author. This method closely resembles the doctrinal approach to the study of Scripture (see chapter 9 of this work).

Since Dr. Tenney has illustrated the former method of performing a topical study, we will use the latter.

*A Different Tack*

In the life of Abraham, we find that, following the events in Genesis 22, Abraham and Sarah lived happily with Isaac for about another twenty years. Then Sarah died (Genesis 23). She is the only woman in the Bible whose age at death is recorded. The significance of this may lie in the fact that God fully compensated her for her long wait for her son to be born.

Genesis 24 is one of the most exquisite pieces of literature in any language. It is beautiful in its simplicity and profound in its description of circumstances, events, and human emotions. No writer, no matter how gifted, can improve on its style or method of communication.

Historically, there is a gap of three years between chapters 23 and 24. When Abraham sensed that the time was right to choose a wife for Isaac, he made the necessary preparations. *"And Abraham said to his servant ... go to my country ... and take a wife for my son Isaac"* (Genesis 24:2-4).

From this simple and direct statement, we immediately discern two important themes: *servanthood* and *marriage*.[1] We can also ask two important questions: What kind of person qualifies for such an important assignment; and equally as important, what qualities will he look for in the woman who is to become Isaac's wife? Both of these topics deserve serious study.

We will take the first, namely, servanthood, as an illustration of one of the methods of pursuing a topical study. As we do so, we must remember that the context, the culture of the times, and the customs of the people are vitally important. Then, as we pursue our investigation, we shall learn a great deal about this servant and how he performed his duties. The procedure we will follow is simple.

As you read over these verses ask yourself, "What is the Holy Spirit revealing to me about this particular topic?" All the pertinent data gleaned from the text, as well as your thoughts and impressions, should be written down in your

---

[1] A third theme, less important in this context than the former two (that comprise the entire chapter), concerns oaths (Genesis 24:2*b*-3).

notebook. No two people will come up with exactly the same list of observations. Here is a sample:

1. Summary statement, vs.1.

2. Servant is not named (though it is generally assumed that he was Eliezer). Faithfulness, not notoriety, is required of a servant. This servant was obviously reliable, for he was in charge of all Abraham owned, vs. 2.

3. He appears to be God-fearing. Note the use of LORD (Yahweh)—implying the God of the Covenant. If he were not God-fearing, such an oath would mean nothing to him,[2] vs. 3.

4. He is prepared to assume a solemn responsibility. The parameters are clearly established, vs. 4.

5. He is sensitive to his master's wishes. He does not need a detailed rationale. He is intelligent and wishes to be cognizant of the issues, vs. 5.

6. Note the specific limitation, vs. 6.

7. Servant is secure in his relationship with his master. He does not misinterpret a warning as a threat. This leaves the channel of communication open for him to *receive encouragement in carrying out his assignment,* vss.6-8.

---

[2] What is the symbolism behind "placing his hand under Abraham's thigh"? Two possibilities have been suggested: (1) that this oath was vitally connected with the perpetuation of Abraham's line and the need for Isaac to take a wife so that he could have children; and (2) failure to perform the oath would incur the anger of God and the servant would be rendered impotent.

8. He willingly undertakes this solemn and responsible task. Fully identifies with what is to be done. Pledges himself to bring about its completion, vs. 9.
9. Servant is prompt in carrying out his master's wishes. There is no unnecessary delay, vss. 10-11.
10. Servant is a man of prayer. He also recognizes his personal needs. He is selfless, and intent on carrying out his commission, vs. 12.
11. Servant entreats God's favor. *"Behold—Lord, see me here, now, and help me,"* vs. 13.
12. Servant is courteous, vs. 17.
13. Servant is patient, watchful, discerning, vs. 21
14. Servant possesses true wisdom. Gives the girl gifts, vs. 22. (Some commentators believe that these were immediately recognized by Rebekah as engagement presents.)
15. Servant is tactful, vs. 23.
16. Servant is thankful for (a) warmth of reception, and (b) God's blessings thus far. Sincere: Bows his head and worships, vs.26.
17. Servant is dignified without being "stuffy." He is humble, yet direct. Provides proof of divine guidance, yet without seeming to "preach" to Rebekah's family, vss. 34-39.
18. Servant is proactive. Handles attempted delay skillfully. Remains in control of the situation. He is also discreet. He does not step outside the boundaries of propriety, vss. 55-58.

19. Servant accomplished his mission. Introduces Rebekah to Isaac. Debriefs so that his master may be in possession of all the facts, vss.65-66.

## *Summing Up*

Once your assessment of the role of a servant in this passage is completed, you can begin to draw together your observations under different headings. This data may come from all parts of the story. It does not (of necessity) have to follow the sequence of the narrative. Here's an example:

*The servant's Godward qualities.* Abraham's servant showed respect for the Covenant. Furthermore, his relationship with God, personal prayer, and worship, all give evidence of a strong Godward relationship (cf. Genesis 24:48).

*The servant's attitude toward authority and authority figures.* He was respectful, loyal, prompt in obedience. He did not shrink from undertaking an important assignment, and he was diligent in carrying out all that had been entrusted to him. He did not serve only when people were watching him. And when with Laban and Betheul, he was confident without being arrogant. This showed that he was inwardly secure.

*The servant's attitude toward himself.* It was healthy; he knew his strengths and weaknesses. He was also cautious, and did not take on something he could not complete. Once he had undertaken the task, he relied on the Lord for help.

He was also secure in his relationship with Abraham. He had worked his way up so that, at this point, he held an honored position in Abraham's household. This shows that he was trustworthy as well as competent.

*The servant's attitude toward his work.* He clearly identified with the task at hand so that his sense of responsibility was maximized, yet his personal worth was not invested in what he was doing so that, if he should fail, he still would not experience a lowered sense of esteem. He was also prayerful. (Not so confident that he believed he could get along without God's help.)

*The servant's plan for carrying out his assignment.* He acted promptly. He was well-prepared (he took with him all the things he might need). Once he arrived in *Paddan-Aram* (the "fields of Aram [or Syria]") he went to the place where he would most likely meet a young girl. (At certain times of the day young women came to draw water out of a well for the needs of the household.) The servant knew about women and the characteristics that would make a good wife; he looked for internal qualities above external beauty. (Rebekah happened to have both.) When he found the girl, he did not delay. He met with her parents, where he was dignified, courteous, and firm. His master's considerations came first. He was always proactive.

*The servant's skill in carrying out his assignment.* His practical wisdom was evident throughout (note verses 33 and 53). His interpersonal relationships with different people show confidence and poise (note conversations in verses 34-49, 54-58). He was persuasive. He was also comfortable with a young girl, with her father and brother, and with her mother.

Upon returning he reported everything to Isaac (verse 66). There was no self-seeking in his report, no "fishing for praise." He debriefed Isaac so that he would know all that had taken place. His report shows his integrity. His disposition was honest; his manner of life above reproach.

## *Turning Point*

With these facts before us, we are now in a position to consult a concordance and a Bible dictionary to find out what else we can learn about servants and servanthood. At first glance we see that the term is used frequently in both Testaments. It is used of the Lord Jesus as the "Servant-Messiah" (see Isaiah 42:1-7; 49:1-9; 50:4-9; 52:13-53:12; 61:1-3). It is also used of a vassal king in relation to his suzerain (II Kings 17: 3). It is used of man being enslaved to sin (Romans 6). It is used of slaves owned by their master (even though in Israel slaves did possess certain rights; see Leviticus 25:39-55; Deuteronomy 15:1-18). And it is used of righteous people in their relationship with God.

A servant was required to obey his master and was dependent upon his master for protection. In turn, he was expected to protect his master's interests. Being a servant gave a person a certain element of security, and many servants were treated so well that they chose to remain with their masters even though they could have been liberated (Exodus 21:1-6).

The term "servant" is also used in prayer (see I Samuel 1:11; II Samuel 7:19ff., 27ff.; Psalm 19:11,13; 27:9; 31:16; etc.), and served to remind the Lord of the dependence of the petitioner upon Him. Scripture also records God's acknowledgment of the allegiance given Him by individuals, and in speaking of them He refers to them as "My servant" (e.g., "My servant Moses" in II Kings 21:8;

Malachi 4:4; see also Numbers 14:24; II Kings 19:34; Job 1:8; Haggai 2:23; etc.). It is hard to escape the fact that *honor* from God is intimately intertwined with the obedience of those who gladly serve Him.

In the New Testament, the usage of the word is the same. It applies to slaves, but also has a spiritual sense implying recognition on the part of the believer that he has been bought by Christ and now belongs to Him. In gratitude, he responds in glad, willing service. Here again the ideas of honor and obedience are intermingled.

In the book of Acts (16:17), Paul and Silas are spoken of as *"servants of the Most High God,"* and Paul unhesitatingly speaks of himself as the *doulos*, "bondslave," of Jesus Christ (see Romans 1:1; Galatians 1:10; Philippians 1:1; Colossians 4:12; etc.). The other New Testament writers do essentially the same thing. This relationship of a redeemed sinner to his Redeemer becomes the foundation of a life of self-effacing service and is characterized by faithfulness, loyalty, steadfastness, and a desire to see one's Master exalted. This is the privilege of every believer.

## *Ample Dividends*

As mentioned earlier, the topical method of Bible study is similar to the doctrinal method. It has certain definite benefits that become apparent to those who are prepared to persevere with it. One of the first of these benefits is the fact that this method of investigating Scripture is very practical. For example, we can begin to study the Christian home and bring together all the material in the Bible on such topics as the home, husbands, wives, fathers, mothers, parents, children, work, in-laws, money, sex, child-rearing, and much more. All the information uncovered will be of practical value.

A second benefit of this kind of study is that it provides us with confidence—the confidence that comes from knowing what God has revealed. As true servants, and with befitting humility, we can then begin to practice what we have learned. In all of our study, we will find that the Lord has carefully balanced each situation in life so that we need not err by going to either one extreme or the other.

The topical method of Bible study is one from which we are able to reap rich rewards. But there are no shortcuts. Diligence is required if accuracy is to be obtained.

## INTERACTION

Having considered the topical method of Bible study in relation to Abraham's servant, now turn our attention to Rebekah and the choice of her as the *bride* of Isaac. By following the procedure outlined in this chapter, you will be able to answer the questions: What qualities did Abraham's servant look for when he set out to choose a bride for Isaac? Was he right? How were these characteristics demonstrated in Rebekah? What other qualities did Rebekah possess? In what ways does the teaching of Genesis 24 apply to us today? (Be sure to note Rebekah's conversations; her delight at being given such impressive gifts [verse 22]; her modesty and discretion in dismounting from her camel and veiling herself before meeting Isaac [verses 63-65]; and her quick adjustment to her husband—sexually and interpersonally [verse 67].)

Chapter Fifteen

# THE FINALE

In his social satire, *Fahrenheit 451*, novelist Ray Bradbury describes a future age in the United States in which it is a crime to own or even to read a book. The barren, regimented lives of the people, the emptiness of their experience, the absence of human values, and the boredom that accompanies the daily, government-controlled forms of entertainment, come across to Bradbury's readers as a frightening prospect of what awaits a nation that has turned its back on the source of its freedom (see John 17:17; cf. 8:32).

Bradbury's story revolves around a fireman, Guy Montag, whose duty it is to burn books found in different homes. Montag, however, saves a book here and there and begins reading them in secret. One day, Montag salvages a copy of the Bible from some books that are to be burned. He vaguely recalls hearing that this book is in some way different from the others, but he knows nothing more about it apart from a few quotations that have become cliches. As he reads, he becomes restless, dissatisfied with the status quo, and prone to question what is happening around him. This arouses suspicion, and in the end he is forced to flee the city.

Bradbury brings *Fahrenheit 451* to a climax when the city from which Montag has fled is utterly destroyed and everyone in it is killed. The ending reminds one of God's heart-rending indictment of His ancient people, Israel. On the eve of their destruction, in words filled with both pity and pathos, He lamented, *"My people perish for lack of knowledge"* (Hosea 4:6).

The similarity between the Israelites and the society that Ray Bradbury describes is striking. Israel was characterized by misplaced confidence, pride, arrogance, and indifference to spiritual realities. In the city of *Fahrenheit 451,* we look into homes where people lead sterile lives, are unable to relate meaningfully to one another, and endure endless banal conversation. They have lost the art of living and exist only because their souls are still united with their bodies. In the end, as with Israel of old, they perish for lack of knowledge. Their demise is at once terrible and tragic, for on the one hand adequate warning could have been given them, and on the other hand they should never have permitted the source of the message of life—namely, God's Word—to be taken from them.

By way of contrast, the Lord, in personifying wisdom as a woman, says:

> *Now therefore, O sons, listen to me,*
> *For blessed are they who keep my ways.*
> *Heed instruction and be wise,*
> *And do not neglect it.*
> *Blessed is the man who listens to me,*
> *Watching daily at my gates,*
> *Waiting at my doorposts.*
> *For he who finds me finds life,*
> *And obtains favor from the LORD,*

> *But he who sins against me injures himself;*
> *And those who hate me love death*
> (Proverbs 8:32-36).

Ray Bradbury concludes his critique of society with those who had been forced into exile banding together and committing to print the content of books that they have memorized. The first work to receive their attention is the Bible. In this connection we need to be continuously reminded that:

> A glory gilds the sacred page
> Majestic like the sun;
> It gives its light to every age,
> It gives, but borrows none.[1]

## *Where We've Been*

In our study of God's Word, we have considered the techniques associated with observation, interpretation, application, and correlation. In doing so we found that these basic approaches underlie all sound Bible study. We also found that once we have mastered these elementary principles, we are in a similar situation to the children in *Sound of Music* whom Maria Von Trapp taught to sing. Once they had learned the tone of "Do, Re, Me ..." et cetera, they could then sing "almost anything." So we, when we have mastered certain basic techniques, are able to read with understanding virtually everything in the Bible.

---

[1] W. Cowper, "The Spirit Breathes Upon the Word," *The Poetical Works of William Cowper,* ed. H. S. Milford (1963), 452.

As our study progressed, we applied different techniques to the record of Abraham and Sarah. These began with synopsis, a bird's-eye view of their life and of God's dealings with them. This preliminary overview, in which we were also introduced to the value of making charts, was then followed by an analytical study based on the Abrahamic Covenant (Genesis 12:1-3).

After this we continued our exposure to different methodologies by assessing the culture of the people of Abraham's time, and we found it necessary to ground our understanding of the teaching of the text within its historic framework. Synopsis and analysis, along with cultural and historical considerations, are basic approaches to the study of any portion of the Bible.

In due course, other methodologies were found to be helpful. These included the geographical, doctrinal, sociological, biographical, ethical, devotional, and topical methods of Bible study. These different approaches were used whenever the content of a passage required them.

Having begun with an overview of Abraham's life, and then having looked at the different parts, it is proper for us to conclude our study with an overview—one in which the parts are put back together again.

At the beginning of our study, you were advised that the information you put into your charts should be regarded as tentative because the perspective you gained as your study progressed would eventually lead you to interpret the content of these chapters in light of the author's theme. But what clues help us to understand what the author (Moses) recorded? Consider, for example, Genesis 12:1, 7; 13:14; 15:1ff.; 17:1ff.; 18:1; 21:1 (Sarah); 21:12; 21:17 (Hagar); 22:1, 15. Each of these passages mentions an appearance of the Lord. And they clearly mark God's progressive revelation.

Initially, therefore, you may wish to structure your outline around the appearances of the Lord to Abraham.

Chapter 14, however, introduces a digression. The kings of the East invade the land and Lot is captured. Of course, Lot's rescue shows that he benefited from the provisions of the covenant. Most important, however, was Abraham's meeting with Melchizedek and his new awareness of the Lord as *El Elyon*, "God Most High." Chapter 16 is another digression. It concerns Ishmael, and the Apostle Paul will later make this the focal point of his discussion of the distinction between legalism and liberty (Galatians 4:21-31). And chapter 19 is yet another digression, this time having to do with the destruction of Sodom and Gomorrah. And so we could go on.

In your chart you can take recurring phrases or themes, and, by using them, piece together the different parts of Abraham's life. In the end, Abraham dies; but only after the Lord has blessed him in everything. You can then survey his entire life—the growth of his spiritual vitality—from his years (possibly as an idolater) in Ur to a man whose life of faith ultimately led to his inclusion in God's "Hall of Fame" (Hebrews 11).

## *Gaining a New Perspective*

But why is it necessary to see this section of Scripture, or any other section, as a whole?

Dr. James Stalker discovered the thrill of reading a book of the Bible through at one sitting. One day, he happened to open God's Word at the book of Romans and read it through without interruption. Later he had this to say about his experience: "I read on and on, right through it. As I proceeded, I caught the spirit of Paul's mighty theme, or rather, was caught by it, and was drawn on to read. The argument opened out and rose like a great work of art above me, till at last I was enclosed within its perfect proportions. This was a new experience. I saw for the first time that a book of the Bible is a complete discussion of a single subject; I felt the full force of the whole argument; and I understood the different parts in the light of the whole as I had never done when reading them by themselves."[2]

We have already listed a few pointers that will help you grasp some of the main seams of Abraham's story. Here are a few additional ideas that will help you gain a more comprehensive understanding of the material.

Read Genesis 11:27-25:11 several times. Let each reading of the material be at one sitting. Each time you read through these chapters, concentrate on a different aspect (e.g., the culture or sociology, development of doctrine, history or geography of the times). Make notes of the ideas that come to mind as a result of your concentration on this specific facet of study. And as you do so, read, learn, and inwardly digest all that God may reveal to you. Then take special note of the covenant and how Abraham's understanding of it was enlarged.

The second time you read entirely through these chapters (preferably on a different day), pay special attention to the development of subordinate topics (the growth of Abraham's faith, references to interpersonal

---

[2] J. Stalker, *The Beauty of the Bible* (1918), 78.

relations, how to handle different human emotions, the way in which God develops a person so that he or she will be able to accomplish His will, God's appearances and methods of revelation, the relationship between obedience and blessing, faith's ability to dispel doubt, etc.).

The next time you read through the entire history of Abraham's life, begin to outline the material in light of the main theme. (These three specifics should not prevent you from further studying the history and geography, customs and culture, et cetera, encountered in these chapters.)

## *Expectations*

Only on rare occasions will the charts of two people agree. Don't let this worry you. In your study you are exposing yourself to God's Word, and whether your choice of words to describe the content of a paragraph agrees with anyone else's is of no importance. Your outline, your chart, and what you derive from this study are all that matters.

But what happens if you come across material in a paragraph that does not fit comfortably into your understanding of the writer's theme? How should you proceed? Here are a couple of suggestions:

- Ask yourself, Have I missed the central purpose of what is recorded? Is it possible that I am working with a subordinate theme? Then review your material.

- Ask yourself, Is my focus too narrow? Have I overlooked something in the main theme that would allow for this material? If so, how can I fit it into my outline?

If the above ideas fail to clarify the issues for you, then reserve judgment on the matter until you have had time to reflect on the passage. For the present, pass over the difficulty and continue with what you are able to do. Then sleep on your problem. This period of "unconscious incubation" will give your mind time to ponder the issues without your being conscious of what is happening. Later on the solution will "suddenly" come to you. So don't be concerned over any imagined lack of expertise. Trust the process, and the rewards will be yours!

## *Words of Encouragement*

Francena H. Arnold is a well-known writer of Christian fiction. She had this to say about her study of Scripture: "I know of no investment of time and effort that will pay higher dividends for life than that spent on Bible study. I am more thankful than I can say that during the years when memorization was easy, and when permanent impressions were being made, I was led to a systematic study of the Scriptures.

"My first course was a simplified survey course in which I learned the names and locations of the different books and a brief, concise statement of the content of each. That was a most valuable first step. The ignorance of the average young person in the fundamental facts of the Bible comes as a shocking surprise to those who are trying to teach them.

"The next course [I took] was a verse-by-verse study of the entire Bible, taken with a class of friends. We were six years on that study, and finally I finished it alone. I

# The Finale 221

found it a most worthwhile and interesting experience. I finished it with a feeling of having acquired a knowledge of the factual content of the Bible, and an understanding of its message and cohesion that I would never lose.

"Since then I have used various methods: Bible doctrine, prophecy, chapter analysis, and many others. From each one I get new truths and new light on an old Book."[3]

Jack Brown is an attorney in Indianapolis, Indiana. His experience was different. This is what he wrote: "The great Apostle Paul admonished young Timothy, *'Study to show thyself approved unto God, a workman who does not need to be ashamed, rightly dividing the word of truth.'* The Greek word for 'study' has a meaning of 'giving diligence,' which emphasizes the importance of careful study in equipping ourselves to *'handle aright'* the Word of God. It is important to have proper materials for our study. In ascertaining the meaning of the Hebrew and Greek words used in Scripture, I have found the following volumes especially helpful to me: *The Expository Dictionary of New Testament Words*, by W. E. Vine;[4] *The Greek Concordance*; *The Amplified Bible*; a good [English] concordance; and a good Bible dictionary.

"To me it is important to know the meaning of the words of Scripture, for we are told, *'All Scripture is given*

---

[3] L. M. Perry and R. D. Culver, eds., *How to Search the Scriptures* (1967), 95-96.

[4] Now issued in one volume as *Vine's Complete Expository Dictionary*, but also containing M. F. Unger's and W. White's Old Testament word studies.

*by inspiration of God'* (II Timothy 3:16) and *'Every word of God is pure'* (Proverbs 30:5) and *'Holy men of God spoke as they were moved by the Holy Spirit'* (II Peter 1:21). The Greek word for 'moved' used here is *phero*, meaning that they spoke as they were borne along by the Holy Spirit, not expressing their own thoughts but the mind of God in words provided and ministered by Him. Since every word of God is pure, every word of God is important and every word of God must be properly understood."[5]

Another man whose life touched thousands of people was the late V. Raymond Edman. A political scientist by training, Dr. Edman later became the president of Wheaton College, Illinois. Before he died, he commented on his use of the Bible. "The Bible is an exhaustless treasure. I read it daily for study purposes to determine the content of each book, then of each chapter, and then the meaning of each verse and word. Apart from this concentrated study of the Word, I read it also for devotional purposes. It is my practice, early in the morning, to read a portion taken consecutively from book to book in the Bible, and read it as it was intended, as God's personal message to me. Thus I find light for the problems of the day, and encouragement to face its difficulties, rebuke for shortcomings and disobedience, warning against self-will, humbling of heart from the Most High. The devotional reading is not for any set length of chapters or verses; rather, the reading may be shorter or longer, depending upon the message from the Word itself. I find that this devotional reading of the Word leads into prayer and praise; and not infrequently what I have learned from the Lord in the early morning devotional

---

[5] *Ibid.*, 101-02.

# The Finale

study of His Word is needed by some other heart before the setting of that day's sun."[6]

## *Where Do You Go from Here?*

Having learned about the different methods of studying God's Word, and having acquired skill in using a concordance and a Bible dictionary, a lifetime of enriching and rewarding experiences awaits you. You may wish to do as the others have done whose testimonies you have just read, and broaden your horizons. As an aid in helping you do this, may I again recommend that you obtain the booklet, *Best Books for Your Bible Study Library* (Loizeaux, 2000), 95pages. It describes the most useful concordances, atlases, dictionaries and Bible commentaries, while also introducing you to those tools that will help you uncover the hidden blessings of God's Word and further stimulate your spiritual growth.

Above all, now that you have gained some experience as an independent student of Scripture, remember the words of the Lord Jesus: *"Every scribe who has become a disciple of the kingdom of heaven [that includes you and me] is like the head of a household, who brings forth out of his treasure [i.e., the riches he has gleaned through his study of the Word] things new and old"* (Matthew 13:52).

And may the Lord richly bless you!

---

[6] *Ibid.*, 91.

## INTERACTION

Bible study begins with an overview of the material to be covered, then analyzes the contents of different sections in different ways, and finally "puts all the pieces together" in the form of a chart. The chart should help you isolate the main movements of the section of Scripture you have studied, highlight the author's main theme, show how he develops it and the way in which each paragraph contributes to the unfolding of his purpose, and give you a complete bird's-eye view of all the material you have covered.

As your final assignment in this study of the principles governing independent Bible study, read over Genesis 11:27-25:11 several times, following the recommendations mentioned in this chapter. Take note of the writer's main theme and observe how he develops it, noting how each paragraph contributes in some way to the unfolding of his purpose. Then make an interpretative chart of these chapters. Remember: No two charts will be exactly alike. Yours will contain your own assessment of the theme and content of the material covering Abraham's life. Finally, do realize that this is just the beginning. These principles can be applied to almost all of Scripture. An exciting future awaits you as you build upon the material covered in this book and, as with Ezra, set yourself to study the law of the Lord, and to practice it, and to teach it to others (see Ezra 7:10).

www.ingramcontent.com/pod-product-compliance
Lightning Source LLC
Chambersburg PA
CBHW070312230426
43663CB00011B/2097